the PURPOSE PRINCIPLE

11 Strategies *to Help You Experience Ultimate Freedom in Your Health, Wealth, and Love Life*

by Kevin Doherty

www.purposeprinciple.com

Mill City Press, Inc.
212 3rd Avenue North, Suite 570
Minneapolis, MN 55401
612.455.2294
www.millcitypublishing.com

ISBN - 978-1-934937-60-0
ISBN - 1-934937-60-6
LCCN - 2008943787

Cover Design and typeset by katzgrafix.com

Printed in the United States of America

To my wife Keri,
for your limitless devotion
and unwavering support.
You are a catalyst for the
expression of my
life purpose.

This book would not have come into being without the help of my wife Keri Signoracci. Her penetrating insight and wisdom permeates every page of this book and she deserves enormous credit for the time, energy, and ruthless honesty she has put into offering creative and editorial input. The book is infinitely stronger because of her generous contribution.

The inspiration I find to initiate and follow through with every single creative endeavor that I embark on these days is largely drawn from my children, Juniper and Ezra. Their presence in my life has been an incredibly powerful catalyst for actualizing my own purpose. They are both sacred teachers to me and I am so grateful that they are a part of my life.

I would also like to thank the many people who read the book and offered invaluable feedback, support, and inspiration. James Roche has been a huge influence in getting this project to move forward with grace and efficiency. Kevin Meddleton, a fellow acupuncturist, has been instrumental in helping me find my authentic voice and keep a consistently inspired tone throughout the book.

I'd also like to thank Joe Dungan for editing the book to make it that much stronger and cohesive and Kat Macconochie, my graphic designer, for always creating the perfect visual representation of my practice and writing.

To my parents, Kay and Pat, for unconditionally supporting my purpose even when it wasn't quite clear how it would all come to fruition.

Lastly, I am deeply grateful to all of the acupuncture patients and coaching clients I've worked with over the past several years. You have all played a significant role in my evolution as an author. Whatever is illuminating about the message of this book has come directly out of my clinical experience working with all of you.

Welcome!

You are about to embark on a deeply meaningful and liberating journey that will help you create the life that you really want. I am absolutely thrilled to be offering this information to you, as this book is the culmination of over 15 years of personal study, struggle, practice, and realization of the strategies taught herein. Since I was a teenager, I have been consumed by the topic of life purpose, primarily because I felt nothing of the sort during that particular phase of development. I intuitively knew from a very young age that my life felt incomplete, like it was lacking something fundamental to the experience of freedom, meaning, and fulfillment.

For much of my life, I felt quite alone in my attempt to understand who I was and why I was here. In fact, my inability to come to terms with the deeper questions of existence was directly related to the extreme shyness, depression, anxiety, and alienation I felt as a young adult. For a reason that remains mysterious, I knew that I had to devote my life to understanding this issue of purpose.

This is why I dove into the study of Western philosophy and psychology at the University of Oregon. I was desperately searching for meaning in my life. I was hell-bent on finding the answer to one simple question: Why am I here?

After three years of frantically searching for the answer to this question, I came to the disappointing conclusion that there was no real solution to be found, at least for me, in the Western worldview. In fact, I felt more confused than ever!

When I was 19 years old, and as my disillusionment with Western philosophy came to a head, a good friend of mine gave me a book called *The Three Pillars of Zen* by Phillip Kapleau Roshi. I read this book in one sitting and almost instantly, my entire understanding of life was irrevocably transformed. Without a shadow of doubt, I knew that I had found something in Zen that directly spoke to my deepest Self. In fact, I vividly remember the uncanny familiarity I felt with the Zen tradition, as if I was remembering a whole universe of truths that I had simply forgotten in this life.

After reading the *The Three Pillars of Zen*, my interest in Asian philosophy took off and I read as many books as I could get my hands on. I also started a daily meditation and yoga practice. It wasn't too long before I realized that I had tapped into my life purpose and that it was time to immerse myself in an environment that would encourage this educational pursuit. On a whim, I dropped out of the University of Oregon and transferred to Naropa University, one of the leading schools for the study of Asian spirituality, meditation, and transpersonal psychology. During this enriching time, I had the good fortune of studying with some of the most evolved and respected teachers in these fields. For the first time ever, I felt settled in myself, like I had finally found what I had been searching for my entire life. In fact, what I essentially experienced through meditation practice was the ability to completely drop the search for anything other than what was presenting itself in the current moment. That was a real eye-opener and radically shifted the way I had been programmed to go about improving my life.

That feeling of peace lasted up until the time I had to take my knowledge out into the world and earn a living. I felt deeply frustrated that there was no laid-out career track before me. Sure, I felt better about myself, but what in the heck was I supposed to do now?

Rather spontaneously, I decided to go to Southwest Acupuncture College to see if I could actually earn a living doing something that genuinely interested me. I got a master's degree in Oriental medicine and then jumped into private acupuncture practice, where I was immediately busy seeing a high volume of patients each week for a variety of physical and emotional health issues. As my practice evolved, I began to realize the importance of helping people at the absolute core of their health concerns, which almost always brought my focus back to the issue of life purpose. Because of this, I decided to offer life coaching in addition to acupuncture.

This book is not only the culmination of my personal journey, but it is also reflective of the finely honed understanding of life purpose that I have gained having worked with hundreds of patients over the past several years.

Without having worked with so many patients, there is no way I could have articulated the strategies behind the Purpose Principle as clearly as I have.

You are now reading what I know to be the perfect summation of my life purpose up to this point along the journey. I hope you find these words as inspiring to read as I have found them to write. I wish you well on this path toward purpose and I encourage you to embrace your own capacity for immediate, profound, and authentic change in any area of your life that deserves it.

Our modern Western civilization is quietly succumbing to an epidemic that is infused with a strong dose of irony. We enjoy more comfort and privilege than any civilization throughout human history, yet our struggle for inner peace and a life of pure health and joy is astonishingly more pronounced than humankind has ever known. We enjoy the many fruits of scientific and technological advancement, yet we are crippled by a host of modern stress-related illnesses that even the brightest medical minds can't cure.

In some ways, life is easier than it's ever been throughout human history. We have easy access to food, entertainment, and virtually any service or resource we desire at the click of a button. What's interesting is that, while life may be getting easier, it is also becoming less simple. It seems that for every advancement we make that is intended to make life more manageable, the collective stress and speed of our society escalates instead of dwindles. While we have the ability to satiate our need for immediate gratification like never before, it is apparent that our collective level of dissatisfaction and struggle is only increasing as evidenced by the staggering number of us who are taking medications for anxiety, depression, and stress-related imbalances.

There is no doubt we are making enormous gains in certain aspects of our development as a species. The question is if our focus has the right foundation to it—that is, are we actually becoming happier, more fulfilled, and more able to connect with the world in a meaningful and authentic way? Or has our attempt at curing the struggles of humanity actually caused this epidemic to run rampant?

And what exactly is this epidemic? We'll get to that in a minute.

*First, I want you to take a look at your own life and
ask yourself the following questions:*

Is there something missing?

Am I completely at peace with who I am?

If I were to die today, would I have any regrets?

Am I totally aligned with the life that I am living in my work, relationships,
finances, and health? Or is there a subtle resistance, a gnawing feeling or
sadness within me that longs for more out of life?

Do I feel like I've tapped into my full potential as a human being and made
a one-pointed commitment to sharing this gift with others?

My hunch is that, up to this point in your life, you have likely done pretty well for
yourself. Perhaps you are even quite successful by conventional standards. But deep
in your heart, if you're really, really honest with yourself, you still know there is
something missing. Sure, you could go on just as you are now. You would be able to
get by and function. Most people would assume that you are doing just fine, that
there is really no problem. But you are ready to make a change. You feel a subtle
tension in yourself that there is more to life than what you have allowed in up to this
point. It may even feel like there is something almost instinctual inside of you that is
longing to surface, but you don't really know what it is or how to express it and you
don't feel too comfortable sharing it with others.

The more you mature and grow as a human being, the stronger this desire for something greater becomes. It begins to feel like an ache deep within your body, a yearn-
ing for a life that taps into a deeper potential within you. It makes you feel restless,
dissatisfied, anxious, or frustrated, or like you can't feel much at all. Sometimes you

take it out on others, while other times it just stays buried in your heart. You feel confused about what this is exactly and what to do about it. As time goes on, it becomes more apparent, however, that this "okay" life you have created for yourself fulfills a mere fraction of your actual potential as a human being. You know there is way more out there for you, but you don't understand where all this is coming from or even if you should listen to it.

Sometimes, when you are in a really quiet place with yourself, it can bring you to tears. Or, once you feel it, you immediately turn away from it and grab the TV remote, plunge back into your work, or call a friend to go out for a movie.

Whether you are 20 or 70 years old, it's likely you experience something like this. You feel a calling within yourself for a better life. It may feel subtle, but it is there. The less distraction there is, the stronger you feel it.

FURTHER SIGNS OF THIS EPIDEMIC

If you can relate to what has been described here, you are certainly not alone. This is the collective experience of countless people who wonder if they are the only ones who feel this. After all, there are millions of people in America alone who are struggling with the following issues and quietly wondering to themselves if anyone else out there can even relate. As you read these, identify how many of these statements resonate for you on a personal level:

- My life feels mediocre. It isn't bad, but I have a sneaky suspicion that it could or should be a lot better.
- While I wouldn't say I'm depressed or even unhappy, I don't really feel a lot of joy and magic in my life either.
- My relationships have repeatedly ended in disappointment or hurt. It seems impossible to find real intimacy.

- I'm stuck in a job that I either don't enjoy or (much more common) one that I can tolerate but that bores me or feels irrelevant to my core values.
- Stress shows up in my life more than I would like and makes me feel "off-kilter."
- I get struck with irrational bouts of anger more often than I'd like.
- I struggle with chronic anxiety or depression and can't figure out why.
- I struggle with addictions: food, cigarettes, drugs, alcohol, caffeine, work, sex, etc.
- My health just isn't where I'd like it to be. I have regular bouts of chronic pain, insomnia, migraines, or other nagging health issues.
- Deep down, I feel insecure about who I am.
- I regularly worry about my finances.
- I never get paid what I'm worth.
- I frequently move to new locations and never seem able to settle; I'm restless.
- I am disorganized or live in chaos.
- My daily life is so busy and hectic that I can never catch up.
- I feel like nobody cares about me.
- I often feel like I don't care about anybody or anything.
- I have tried to change myself for the better, but always end up in the same frustrating place.
- I am caught in feelings of negativity or pessimism.
- I feel bored a good amount of the time.
- I can never seem to figure out what I want to do with my life.
- I have unfulfilled dreams.
- I make excuses as to why I can't have or be anything I wish.
- My life feels random and meaningless.
- I sleep excessively or I have a hard time falling or staying asleep.

- I often feel that I have to "suck it up" and do things that I don't really want to do, like this is the only way to feel like I'm a good person.
- I know that I procrastinate in living my true dreams and passions; I crave more from life but I'm not sure what to do about it.
- I feel stuck where I am.

THE REAL ISSUE EXPOSED

You can probably identify a few things from this list that you have struggled with. So, what core issue, what mounting epidemic are all of these symptoms pointing to?

A lack of purpose.

This is the main problem facing our modern world. We have simply lost touch with who we are and why we are here. Because of this, we are unwell. Sure, we are getting by and doing okay. We are able to survive. We are not starving. We feel comfortable. But we are not fully alive. There is a fundamental part of our being that has gone missing. We could call this our Spirit, awareness, essence, or true nature. The terminology isn't what matters. What does matter is that you discover how to get this part of yourself back. That is what this book is about.

When we lack purpose, we will be stuck in survival mode. We will never feel fully at peace and deeply fulfilled. Perhaps one aspect of life, such as our health or our work, will appear to be successful, but the WHOLE picture will max out at mediocrity. Without purpose, we can never go beyond "middle of the road."

Does it have to be this way? Absolutely not. In fact, you can change it right now. The rest of this book will show you how. Indeed, there is a sacred reason that you have been brought to this material at this time in your life. Whether this book has been brought to you due to this subtle feeling that you want more out of life, or you are someone that has experienced incredible hardship, you are here because you are ready to stop doubting yourself and to start actively creating the life that you really want.

Since 2001, I have owned a holistic health practice where I do acupuncture, herbal medicine, nutrition, and life coaching, and teach meditation and yoga. Having worked with hundreds of patients for various health and lifestyle issues, I've come to the overwhelming realization that our modern culture is in dire need of purpose. What has become crystal clear to me is that so many of us feel that we are all alone in our suffering; we feel that nobody can understand what we are going through. We feel that our suffering is unique. What I have witnessed in the healthcare setting suggests the exact opposite: So many of our problems are strikingly similar. In fact, I have on many occasions been amazed by the astonishingly high percentage of my patients whose various health issues could be traced back to this core issue of lacking life purpose.

The premise of this book is quite simple but radical in its implication: *Uncover and commit to your purpose in every aspect of your life, and you will achieve a level of wellness and freedom that you currently can't even conceive of.* To feel and be well, you must have purpose. Wellness is the ultimate antidote to mediocrity, the ultimate cure for this epidemic that plagues our modern world. Wellness is a state of being fully plugged into who you are, being in the zone, fully awake and alive. It is a proactive state of being where you live at the edge of your personal greatness. It encompasses the totality of your life, from your physical, emotional, and spiritual health to your work, finances, and relationships.

WHAT IS THE PURPOSE PRINCIPLE?

The Purpose Principle is the actual foundation of life purpose itself; it is a formulaic way of accessing the sacred dimension of your life in all areas. The Purpose Principle is really a unique synthesis of the various ancient wisdom traditions[1], which universally agree that life purpose is the core influence that determines how much wellness we have in relation to every theme and dimension of our experience as human beings. It is our gateway to a sacred life of fulfillment that transcends mediocrity and disease. It is the ultimate source of freedom that underlies our health, love life, finances, job, parenting, and every other dimension of life.

Admittedly, exposing the silent epidemic of purposelessness may sound like a grim way to open this book. The good news is that you can activate the Purpose Principle starting right now. You have access to ultimate freedom in this very moment. It does not take time nor does it require a tremendous amount of work. All it really takes is a willingness to change. Having taken many people through a healing process in my acupuncture and life coaching practice, this is one of the most liberating and profound realizations that I can offer to you in this book: Change happens now. It is possible.

You don't need to spend twenty years in therapy trying to process through all of your traumas. You don't need to travel to Tibet to find something that you feel isn't within you already. Even if you are $50,000 in credit card debt, in a troubled marriage, hate your job, or are 100 pounds overweight, your innate essence is still perfect. Ironically, healing the imbalances in our life is based on the recognition that there is this complete part of us that doesn't need to be healed at all. When we identify with this place, our outer life begins to shift in a very natural, almost effortless way.

The strategies[2] mentioned in this book will be brought to life by real examples and case studies of patients going through remarkable and quick change through our work together in my practice. Know that the same is possible for you. Changing the epidemic of purposelessness and mediocrity begins on an individual level. You are reading this book because it is your turn to "be the change that you want to see in the world" as Gandhi so eloquently put it. It is your turn to infuse your life with purpose and create a level of wellness that will inspire others to do the same.

THE BEGINNER'S MIND

In the beginner's mind there are many possibilities, in the expert's mind there are few.
— Suzuki Roshi

It is time to start over. Wipe the slate clean. In order to be moved by the messages within the forthcoming strategies, you'll need to do away with much of what you have been taught about who you are and how to be a good, responsible person. Put aside everything that you know about how life is. Be willing to hang out in some unknown territory.

As you embark on this new learning process, pretend that you are back in school and have not as of yet absorbed all kinds of information about who you are and how life is. Your mind is still empty. When it comes to learning about life purpose, this is a very helpful way to begin. You see, the first seven strategies that form the foundation of the Purpose Principle are the most important teachings you should have learned growing up. Without these strategies deeply integrated into your life experience, you will inevitably find yourself struggling to become the person you really want to be. You will endlessly ask yourself, "Is this all that life has to offer?"

You'll find yourself experiencing a vague sense of dissatisfaction, even when you achieve certain goals or have positive experiences.

These strategies are combined together with the intention of being a practical, step-by-step guide to bringing about authentic change in your life. Even if you have been frustrated or have given up hope that your life can be immensely more fulfilling and wonderful, these strategies can trigger a natural awakening into the life you really want.

There are no quizzes, but you will be tested by your life every day to see if you are committing to this material.

You may have come across several or all of these 11 strategies before. In truth, each of these strategies has been taught since the dawn of human civilization. The problem that many of us face is that we *know* these teachings but don't feel that we can act on them. We struggle to implement them into reality. In fact, you may be someone who has devoured a tremendous amount of self-help literature. You could even teach your own class on self-improvement. But the information hasn't led to real-life changes. Many people find that the more they read and try to "work" on themselves, the worse they feel. Why? Because their inability to implement what they have learned makes them feel like a failure. If this has been you, this frustrating process seems to offer irrefutable proof that you are uniquely exempt from a life of fulfillment and joy. After all, wouldn't you have "gotten it" by now?

THE PROBLEM IS TWOFOLD

1 The self-help material you have studied has been very inspirational, but hasn't really given you a step-by-step system for making authentic change and fulfilling your purpose every day that you live.

2 While you may have intellectually understood much of what you've learned, you simply haven't been ready to integrate it into reality.

The strategies you are about to learn are intended to help you with both of these issues. By the end of this book, it is imperative that you feel empowered to act upon what you have learned. After all, the whole point of the information you are about to absorb is that you actually experience ultimate freedom instead of just learn about it. There is a big, big difference between concept and experience. Implementing what you are about to learn into your life boils down to your ability to embrace the following statement...

The only moment you have is now

When you realize this, you will be ready to take action. If this truth eludes you, you will tell yourself something to the effect of "hmm, that's interesting" and nothing will happen, or you will use this material as further evidence that you are incapable of changing yourself for the better.

Much of what you are about to learn will give you a radically new orientation for creating the life that you really want. This orientation is largely about dropping any resistance you may have to claiming your life purpose, including your current way of "working on yourself." As you will learn, your way of trying to improve yourself is often a big part of the problem (the fifth strategy is all about this). I have written this book with a keen sensitivity to the potential pitfalls that you may face as you attempt to integrate these strategies into your life. My hope is that you feel empowered to put the Purpose Principle into action and make these strategies the top priority for each day that you live.

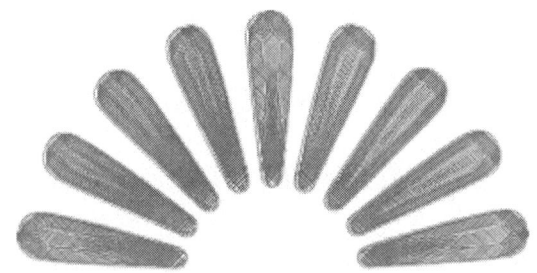

As mentioned, identifying and expressing your life purpose is the only way to experience wellness, abundance, and thriving health. Since life purpose is at the foundation of each strategy we'll be covering, it's imperative that you are clear about what life purpose is and what it is not. This overview will create a solid foundation, as simply understanding what life purpose is can be immensely helpful and liberating.

There are two definitions of life purpose that we will use to understand and integrate the following 11 strategies:

1 **An awareness of present moment reality**
2 **The identification and expression of our innate gifts, heartfelt aspirations, and limitless potential**

We will be referring to these two definitions throughout this book. It will become clear that the first definition always serves as a gateway to the second definition. This means that our ability to identify and express our genuine strengths and passions is based on how anchored we are in the present moment. If that sounds confusing, don't worry about it. This point will become very clear as you progress through these strategies.

Let's look at a few other main attributes of life purpose, as it can be defined and discussed in a variety of ways.

LIFE PURPOSE IS

- ◪ A resource of strength and wisdom that is innate to your makeup as a human being. It has been with you since day one, even if you have never made contact with it or felt its presence. It is what propels you forward in life, keeping you in a constant state of growth and movement. It is what frees you up to be your real Self, to tap into all of your incredible potential. It is as much a state of your being as it is what you do with your life. Your life purpose has been with you always. It is never, ever foreign or external to you. It is innate to your makeup.

- ◪ What enables you to see every experience, good, or bad, as a lesson that can help you evolve.

- ◪ Always waiting peacefully and patiently within you, no matter how far or often you stray from it. It is always with you and always will be.

- ◪ What brings meaning, depth, and substance to your life. Life purpose is a bridge that connects you fully with the world. It is the combination of innate attributes you possess that naturally uplift, excite, and awaken both you and the entire world. Life purpose is the role you have in the cosmic play. It is your unique script. It lies at the core of your being and can never be damaged or eradicated. It is the exact reason you took birth in a human body and decided to incarnate as your exact Self.

- ◪ Your direct gateway to serving and helping others. It is your unique expression of who you are and a means of conveying that expression out to the world for the greater good. Life purpose is always about serving others. Deep within you—within each of us—there lies an authentic and heartfelt desire to offer the very best within you to the world. This source of wisdom and meaning is here to help in whatever way it can. It has no self-concern and is totally committed to the greater good. It is a refuge of freedom, a path away obsession and narcissism. It is your direct vessel of service. It is an invitation to extend yourself to the world so that your life becomes an offering to others. It is seeing that you are here not for your own self-concern but for the greater good of the planet and the universe. It is what takes you out of a narrow focus on yourself and lands you in the lap of universal consciousness. Life purpose is the vehicle you choose to bring out your fullest expression of humanity and service to the world.

- What makes you feel connected to the universe. Life purpose fills you with the inseparability of all living things. It is what enables you to see that you are not separate from the outside world. Life purpose is the sole source of wholeness within you. It is a one-pointed, very direct way of being in the world. It is what arises when you are in direct contact with the source of your life—the mysterious, incomprehensible forces around and within you. It is your link to infinity and eternity.

- A calling to fulfill your full potential starting right now. Your purpose recognizes no limitations. It is the voice within you that says YES to life, that is fully committed to the here and now and eager to help others find their own voice.

- The process of living intentionally. This is the opposite of living habitually, where we don't have a direct relationship with the moment-to-moment reality of our lives. When our life purpose is activated, we are engaged in an ongoing dialogue with the universe. We can sense the infinite universe within our own skin and we feel a calling to extend our very best to anyone and everything that needs us. We activate this calling through conscious intention.

- The process of cultivating a conscious relationship with yourself and life in general. It is about living in awareness and power. It is the fulfillment of your deepest dreams and the absolute nourishment of your core spiritual desires. When we live with purpose, we wake up. Our entire Self is ready for life, right here and now.

- What opens you up to a reality that is much larger than the one that keeps you bottled up in yourself. Life purpose is what makes us feel like we are floating a few inches off the ground. It is the source of human exultation, enthusiasm, and joy. It brings us in contact with the infinite and eternal nature of the cosmos.

- The very basis of altruism and generosity

- The nurturing of what we are the very best at and what we love doing the most.

- Often born out of the adversity we have faced.

- The basis of spiritual, emotional, and financial prosperity

REAL-LIFE EXAMPLES OF
THE PURPOSE PRINCIPLE

- You lose yourself in something that you are doing and ten hours have felt like five minutes.

- You realize you have a personal genius for something that you don't see too often in others.

- You offer to help someone and realize that, in the process of helping, a feeling of joy and connection has welled up within you. It becomes apparent that you are being helped by helping others.

- You suddenly remember a childhood dream you had that has gone unfulfilled and you feel an enormous surge of motivation to make that dream reality.

- You realize that if you weren't involved with _____, you would not want to be alive.

- Out of a place of pure silence and surrender, your mind fills with new and provocative images that guide you toward a certain action.

- You are able to look back at your life and sincerely appreciate the contributions you have made to the lives of others. You have no regrets.

- Even though you have had countless people telling you how to live your life, you listened to your own voice and never looked back. The people that doubted you have come to admire you.

- Every day feels brand new. You are able to bring a creative energy to every facet of your life.

- You find yourself in a constant state of fascination, amazed by the mysterious wonders of the universe and how all of this came into being.

- Even when life has dealt you challenges, you have been able to draw upon a source of inner resiliency that enables you to gracefully handle any potential obstacles.

- You find yourself more interested in activities that require your fullest aptitude than you are in immediate gratification.

- You bring a quality of loving presence to everything that shows up in your reality; nothing is ignored or seen as unworthy of your care.

OK, now that we know what life purpose is, let's contrast that with what it is not.

LIFE PURPOSE IS NOT

- At all aligned with beliefs or activities that promote violence, scarcity, separation, suffering, or destruction. It is an incredibly life-affirming presence within each of us that only wishes to help.

- Tied up in any sort of doctrine, dogma, or religion.

- An esoteric concept that is only relevant to adherents of New Age metaphysics.

🔲 Based on secular beliefs about who we are, nor does it conform to the conventional roles that we feel we must abide by.

🔲 Some sort of abstract concept that requires us to be really smart in order to comprehend. Ironically, the most clever and smart people are often the ones who have the hardest time contacting their life purpose because they are blocked from the pure simplicity and naturalness of it.

🔲 Necessarily related to our talents or what has made us feel successful up to this point in life. When a talent is identified within us, we are often pushed in the direction of utilizing or exploiting it in order to be successful. Whenever we are being fueled by the voice of "should," will power, guilt, fear, or anxiety, or we feel that we have to push in order to get what we want, we are missing our purpose. Whenever we feel that we just have to "suck it up" and deal with our life, it is a surefire sign that we are blocked from our purpose. Each one of us has many different talents. Some people have been encouraged to develop their talents so they can wear them as adornments that command respect and adoration, while for others, their talents remain dormant within them. Life purpose is not about forcing the development of certain talents as a way to success.

🔲 Something that requires will power, force, or even hard work. In fact, these qualities often serve as direct obstacles to purpose. When your purpose is activated, you will likely work harder than you ever thought possible, but at that point you would not even call it work in the conventional sense of the term. It is simply what you are here to do.

🔲 Confined to your job and can't really be defined by what you do. It is more about who you are. In this sense, your life purpose is expressed through every facet of your life: your job, relationships, finances, diet, exercise patterns, and so on. You bring a sense of purpose to every dimension of life and to all that you do. In fact, in order for your purpose to reach its fullest expression, it needs to shine through all of the little details of your life. If one piece is left out, then an aspect of your purpose will remain blocked. For instance, if you love your job and feel deeply nourished and excited by it, but your marriage is suffering because you work too much, then your purpose is still being suppressed to some extent. It needs to flow through you in every dimension of life. It can't arise in one aspect of life to the exclusion of others.

- Related to how much money you make or the extent of your material acquisitions. There are purpose-driven people who live very modestly and make just enough money to get by, while there are other purpose-driven people who are billionaires.

- Something that we merely believe in. It is not something that can only come into being when certain conditions are met. Its presence within us does not depend on external factors whatsoever.

- Capable of surfacing when your focus is on your problems and what you don't want.

Now we have clearly defined what life purpose is and what it is not. The rest of this book will give you practical and inspiring solutions for stepping out of distress, mediocrity, and fear and into a life of meaning, fulfillment, and true wellness. I invite you to immerse yourself in the following 11 strategies so you can experience the Purpose Principle in your life starting NOW.

Section I

THE FOUNDATION
of the
Purpose Principle

The bulk of this book is dedicated to this first section, as it will serve as a foundation of wisdom upon which you must build every aspect of your life. This foundation truly is the missing link for so many of us. The first seven strategies that make up this section will give you a radically new and refreshing understanding of how to make authentic change in any area of your life. This combination of strategies is a proven formula that will show you how to live in power, grace, and harmony if you follow it with 100% commitment.

In section II, we will apply this foundation to all of the main areas of your life. The key is that you implement this formula so it becomes second nature in a way that is similar to every breath you take. It is indeed a practice that requires ongoing training and refinement. The good news is that every moment of every day gives you ample opportunity to practice this formula!

In section III, we'll examine how life looks when your purpose comes to full fruition. As you will come to learn, this is in no way a remote ideal. You have access to the fruition of life purpose in this moment.

Let's start with the first part of this foundation,
which is knowing that you have a sacred purpose.

KNOW That Your Life Has a Sacred Purpose

If you bring forth what is within you,
What you bring forth will save you.
If you do not bring forth what is within you,
What you do not bring forth will destroy you.

—Jesus, from The Gospel According to Thomas

TAKE A LOOK AT THE FOLLOWING STATEMENTS

⦿ *The fact that you are here means that you matter. There is a sacred purpose to your existence.*

⦿ *Your life is precious beyond words.*

⦿ *Inside of you is a vast reservoir of potential that must be contacted and expressed if you are to ever experience lasting fulfillment.*

⦿ *Once this potential is unleashed, there is absolutely no limit to what you can be, do, or have.*

⦿ *True power is found within. It is the power of your purpose. The more you serve others, the more this power is activated.*

⦿ *Activating your purpose means that you are fully aware that every thought, feeling, intention, and action has a consequence. You can't get away with anything.*

⦿ *You have an inner genius that is the unique combination of innate gifts you possess.*

⦿ *You are a miracle. Your life is a reflection of the divine mystery of the universe.*

What is your first reaction upon reading these statements? If you are like the vast majority of people in our modern world, you were never taught these universal truths growing up. Undoubtedly, you were taught a variety of other useful things, but the truths that ultimately determine how content and balanced you are and how profoundly you can leave a positive imprint on the world have been largely ignored. Doesn't that seem strange to you?

In fact, it is more than strange. It is a tragedy beyond measure. Without a deep connection to these purpose-based statements, our lives will inevitably be full of undesirable qualities like mediocrity, conflict, and struggle. These kinds of teachings are the ones that matter the most. Integrating these statements into our daily framework of being is the most crucial element to healthy emotional and spiritual development, not to mention a thriving work, financial, and love life. Unfortunately for most of us, this element has either been largely ignored or altogether dismissed based on the way we are educated and conditioned. We can define conditioning as the various teachings and examples that we absorb from the influences around us that determine what we believe to be true about life. It is assumed that these matters are handled by our religious institutions, but many of us have had the experience of religion being a direct obstacle to the actual nurturing of these truths within ourselves.

By the time we hit adulthood, is it any wonder that so many of us question why the hell we're here? Or why we just can't seem to find a job that we like? Or why we end up playing out the same old traumas and dramas in our relationships? Or why we get the nagging feeling that we're skimming the surface of our true potential? Or why we never feel complete in ourselves, as if this moment is totally okay the way it is? Or why we struggle with low energy, chronic health problems, and incessant worry?

It is because this crucial element has been absent, which means the foundation of the Purpose Principle was never laid.

WHO WOULD YOU BE IF...

Can you imagine how different your life would be if the truth of these statements were nurtured within you since the time you were born? What if you were in first grade and the first lesson the teacher offered you was on life purpose? What if all of the facts and figures you had to learn were backed by an understanding of how this information directly applied to the unfolding of your innate gifts? And how amazing would it have been to know that, if the information wasn't directly relevant to your unique development, then you simply didn't have to waste your time with it? What if your parents were living examples of these purpose-based statements? What if they taught you these truths through their actions and words? Can you see how your entire experience as a child who is learning what life is and how it works would have been radically shifted? How might this have affected you as an adult? Do you think you would be in the same job, marriage, financial situation, or level of health that you're in now? Who knows, maybe your life wouldn't have been any easier, but you can probably see how this kind of foundation would have given you a shortcut to learning the life lessons that allow you to evolve and succeed.

A DEEPER LOOK AT THE EPIDEMIC

If you take a look at the state of the modern world, it is clear that there is a collective human need to explore and experience these truths. When we aren't in direct connection with who we really are, why we are here, and what we really want, we are subjected to a life of struggle, mediocrity, and stress. We get sick.

Our relationships suffer. We turn to other people to fill this place of emptiness within ourselves. We succumb to various addictions such as alcohol, sugar, drugs, shopping, or sex in order to fill this void. We spend our lives desperately trying to feel better. We crave validation from others. Our relationship with ourselves is plagued by insecurity, doubt, fear, and confusion. We don't know which voice to listen to within ourselves or how to make decisions in the right way based on what we really need. Instead, we flounder. We either move through life impulsively or we are overly conservative.

Realizing that something isn't quite right, we turn to various external sources to give us answers and solutions. We go to medical doctors, therapists, healers, weight loss centers, and other sources of relief. We try to make ourselves feel better by doing what we know how to do to "take the edge off." The real source of our disease, however, remains obscured.

For many of us, the signs of being blocked from our purpose are more subtle. We are getting through life seemingly well. All things on the outside point to a successful life. We can have a good job, nice house and car, stable finances, a good marriage, and so on, but still feel like something is missing. Often times, we can't pinpoint what it is that's missing, but we vaguely sense a feeling of emptiness, like there is a soft voice whispering deep within our heart, "Is this all that I can expect of my life?" For some of us, the main sign of being blocked from purpose is boredom. We feel uninspired. Life has become a "ho hum" routine rather than a vibrant and dynamic process. It's not that we are miserable or even unhappy. It's just that we feel kind of "blah" about the whole affair. We feel uneasy about the possibility of living this way forever, but we're not really sure how to change it or if we really even want to change it.

CASE STUDY ⚮ **KATHLEEN** ⚮

Kathleen came to my acupuncture practice after taking several rounds of antibiotics for recurring lung infections. Her immune system was quite weak, as she was vulnerable to regular bouts of cold and flu-like symptoms. Kathleen also mentioned that her stress level was quite high and that she had been in a job for 12 years that never felt like the right fit. All signs on the outside pointed to an attractive, intelligent, and successful woman who was doing all the right things in her life. On the inside, however, it was clear that Kathleen felt an emptiness in her life.

Though she stayed fit and ate well, she had lost much of the vitality that she enjoyed in her youth. She felt unfulfilled in her life even though all of her friends and colleagues assumed she was happy and successful. Kathleen's core issue was that she was lacking purpose. Her work was meaningless to her and did not align with her deeper strengths and gifts, even though she was very good at it and was financially compensated quite well.

Kathleen committed to a series of acupuncture and life-coaching sessions that gradually transformed her from the inside out. She became increasingly empowered in her conviction that she was meant to take her business background and help business owners succeed using spiritual principles.

continued

Kathleen came in for treatment one day and excitedly announced that she had given notice at her job. Everyone she worked with looked at her like she was crazy. They couldn't believe she was willing to let go of a high-paying job that many in her industry would have killed for.

What her colleagues didn't realize was that Kathleen had made a fundamental shift in her consciousness that simply did not align with the work she was doing. She was destined to find an outer role to play that matched her newly found expansive view of herself and her reality. After coming to these realizations and quitting her job, Kathleen's health made dramatic improvements. Her immune system became instantly stronger, her energy level was much higher, and her emotional life felt much more balanced.

These profound and swift changes occurred because Kathleen was willing to consider the possibility that her life held a sacred purpose that wasn't being fulfilled.

When our purpose is blocked, we feel like a victim to the whims of fate, never quite sure how to navigate through the whirlwind of each day. Things feel unworkable and out of sync. For many of us, this is how we define stress: A consistent feeling of contraction, tension, and resistance. By and large, this modern epidemic we call stress is really just a label we give to being out of alignment with our life purpose. When we feel like the outer world is dictating the course of our life, we will naturally perceive life as an out-of-control and random process that sets the stage for stress.

When we are aligned with our purpose, it's like our lives happen in a state of flow. We are finally swimming with the current of life instead of constantly resisting it. We no longer use will power and force to push our way through life. Instead, there is a natural source of effortlessness that guides us through each moment. This effortlessness is based on an inner knowledge that we can always meet our outer circumstances with grace and awareness; nothing that happens on the outside can beat us down. By recognizing that we have a purpose, we are simultaneously recognizing that we have a responsibility to this life to bring the absolute best within us to the surface. We see that we have an enormous influence in the circumstances that show up, as if we are actually magnetizing things to us based on our perceptions of what is true. When we make this link between our inner and outer reality, we are closing the door once and for all on placing blame, making excuses, or settling for less than the full expression of our purpose.

To answer this question, let's return to our two definitions of life purpose.

1 **An awareness of present moment reality.** Your primary purpose as a human being is to be fully aware of what is happening in this very moment. All of your senses are engaged with your present experience. We will explore this concept in much more depth in the second strategy.

2 **The identification and expression of our unique gifts, heartfelt aspirations, and limitless potential.** By keeping your awareness focused on the present moment, you have access to what is unique about your offering to this planet. You see that you have been created to identify and offer something that only you could; it is totally unique to you based on your specific conditions, genetics, and spiritual makeup. Whatever this core offering is that you have to make to the world, *you MUST bring it forth in order to experience ultimate freedom and wellness.*

To put it simply, expressing your purpose to the world is the only reason you are here. Everything else is a distant second. If you commit to this, your life will flourish.

Realizing that you have a sacred purpose has much deeper and broader implications than your personal fulfillment. Indeed, the existence of our planet hinges upon each individual's understanding of their purpose. If we are connected with our purpose, then we will treat all forms of life with reverence and do our best to be of service. Because we realize the interconnectedness of all forms of life, the welfare of the whole becomes our top priority. Life purpose means that we are filled with a strong will not only to live, but to be fully alive. When it is activated, this will extends to all of humanity and to the planet as a whole. Put simply, in order for our planet to survive, we must blow apart the narrow parameters of self-concern and put the power of purpose into full throttle.

Identifying the problem of living without purpose can feel like a heavy issue. Ironically, when we allow our purpose in, all the heaviness of life is lifted from us. We see that there is a very light, playful quality to our nature that has remained unscathed by the layers of beliefs that make life feel like a heavy experience. Life purpose is what lifts us out of the self-imposed boundaries of separation and helps us unite with a much larger reality than anything we have known. It is our direct link back to infinity. It is the force within us that is unified with the beginningless and endless nature of time and space. It is what activates our capacity to offer love and beauty to others. Doesn't it make sense that your life will thrive if you have a deep reverence for the reason why you showed up here in the first place? And that you will always feel restless and alienated if you ignore your purpose?

Our modern world has, by and large, forgotten the absolute importance of this kind of inquiry into ourselves. We have taken a detour that has kept us traveling down a path of endless distraction. Sure, we're learning more about the external universe; we're making more discoveries and advances in science, technology, and medicine. But we have strayed from our inner universe, the one that ultimately defines how much fulfillment and magic we are able to discover and create.

THE SPECTRUM OF INFINITE POTENTIAL
WHERE DO YOU LAND?

Fig. 1.1–

INFINITE POTENTIAL

JOY, FREEDOM, AND GENEROSITY—

While accessible to each of us, perhaps only 1% of humanity consistently lives at this end of the spectrum.

THE VAST MAJORITY OF US ARE HERE

Mediocrity—Life is OK, could be better but could be worse, typified by a quiet and subtle longing for more out of life, putting off what really matters.

MISERY~DESPAIR~ANGUISH

This diagram offers a visual representation of where the vast majority of modern people are at in relation to the spectrum of human potential. At the bottom of this spectrum are the basest forms of human life that revolve around qualities like misery, despair, and anguish. The range where most of us are taught to identify with is certainly above these base qualities, but far below our infinite potential. Typical states of being that summarize our life experience within this range are:

- I'm doing okay
- It's not that I'm unhappy
- Life is pretty good
- It's not like I feel bad about myself
- I'm fine
- It could be worse
- I should feel better about my life; after all, most people have it much worse than I do
- I know I need to ___, but I just don't have the time, am not quite ready, and/or am not sure I can do it

At the top of this spectrum in a never-ending line is our infinite potential that brings forth the most charged and powerful states of being that we can have, such as limitless joy, freedom, and generosity. Most of us don't see how we are blocked from our purpose. We assume that feeling "fine" is about all we can ask of life.

Learning that your life has a purpose is certainly an individual process that does not have a textbook format that you can follow. While it is true that many of us learn that we have a purpose only after we have endured a certain degree of adversity and hardship, the crucial point here is that we don't prolong our suffering longer than necessary to get this lesson. This means that, once you get the lesson, it is time to move on. Don't stay in a failing marriage for another 30 years thinking that there is another life lesson to be had from enduring such struggle. All it takes is an initial wake-up call, then it's time to get out. Most of us have an incredibly high tolerance for situations and relationships that we should have let go of long ago.

You will know that your life has a purpose when you are ready to know this. The third strategy, being willing to putting your purpose first, will explore this in much more depth.

For many of these strategies, I will offer a Q &A format that addresses the most common questions I have heard in my years of clinical practice along with practical exercises that you can work with to bring what you are learning into your direct experience.

Okay, that's a lot of information. Any questions before we move on?

What went wrong? Why do so many of us struggle to embrace a life of meaning, inspiration, and joy? Why do we feel so disconnected and fragmented? Even if our feelings don't seem that extreme, why do we often feel a subtle sense of dissatisfaction, a gnawing kind of discontent or friction with our lives?

You see, the problem for so many of us is that we never learned how to utilize our spiritual instincts and intuition from a very young age so that we could always stay in contact with our purpose. While you may have learned a lot in the various schools you have attended, the chances are slim that you ever learned how to identify and express your life purpose to the world and commit to this process as the top priority in your life. Instead, you were taught a lot of facts and figures, and a lot about other people's viewpoints and beliefs. You were also taught that you should seek security at all costs, that the attainment of a predictable and secure reality is the most coveted quality and top priority in life. The problem is that this quest leaves almost no room for our life purpose to be expressed. When we are taught to put security before anything else, what is running the show? Usually fear and obligation. We believe that we should pursue a certain role or career in life and that we should choose this for the money, the status, the social acceptance, whatever it is.

Our life purpose has nothing whatsoever to do with "should," or will power, which can be defined as forcing our way through life out of fear. It is a radical departure from the life of routine security and idle comfort. It is not at all based in habitual actions or beliefs that keep us feeling half-alive. Life purpose is all about becoming free in your life—free from harmful beliefs, negative emotions, addictions, stagnant jobs, or anything else that feels burdensome, stressful, or painful. Life purpose is about freedom. It is about tapping into your authentic Self and fully expressing this to the world in each moment. We can't simultaneously embark on a quest for freedom and security. We have to choose which one is more aligned with our core values. Do you want to be fully alive and free or do you want to stay safe and comfortable?

We learn the most important life lessons from our most immediate influences, namely our parents and teachers. And we tend to learn a lot more from what they do as opposed to what they say. The actions of those closest to us serve as the most direct influence in forming our beliefs about who we are and why we're here. Therefore, if we grew up in a house where our parents displayed constant anxiety and worry because money was always tight, it is highly likely that we will internalize their actions and form an understanding of money based on their influence. In this sense, most of us pretty much reenact through the course of our lives what we have learned from those closest to us.

We live in a society that bombards us with surprisingly powerful messages as to who we should be and how we should live. As our schools, churches, and parents lead us through example during our childhood, the media, the government, and various social institutions do the same for us as we enter adulthood. Unfortunately, many of the messages we absorb are diametrically opposed to the fulfillment of our life purpose. Many of us find that these messages tend to promote the notion that the power is "out there," which causes us to clutch to anything that makes us feel secure, immediately gratified, or validated.

Simply put, most of us have encountered very strong layers of conditioning from our most fragile and impressionable stages of development as children all the way through the process of maturation into adulthood. We are bombarded with external messages that block us from contacting this innate source of wisdom and power that resides within each of us.

Why do we avoid the topic of life purpose?
Why don't we learn all of this growing up?

Good question. In many other parts of the world, life purpose is the central focus of human development. This understanding is skillfully infused into children and encouraged to develop as the guiding force into adulthood. Now, this can only happen when the culture's viewpoint is geared toward an appreciation of the interconnectedness of life, the invisible reality that lies beyond our physical world, and the important contribution that each Spirit has to make to the betterment of the planet. When a culture is steeped in this kind of wisdom, life purpose is the natural focus of all stages of human development.

Our modern societies, on the other hand, have largely embraced a viewpoint that is focused almost exclusively on materialism and an obsession with the need for personal gain due to a feeling of separateness and aloneness. When we don't feel an inseparable connection to the universe and all of its various life forms, we will by default operate out of fear. Our value system will be one that emphasizes the need for personal security beyond all else. We attain this security through acquisition, force, and hard work. This worldview has been handed to us by the greatest thinkers of the modern era such as Isaac Newton and Rene Descartes, who pioneered the belief that the physical world is the end-all be-all of life. The reigning conclusion of our visionary forefathers: What can't be apprehended by our five senses or proven through logic and scientific scrutiny should not be seen as useful or valid.

Most of our social, psychological, and religious values have sprung out of this rather compromised way of understanding reality. The result is that most of us are taught from day one to focus on protecting our personal territory and ensuring our basic survival. Even though we may have been raised in a loving and supportive environment, we are taught through the various media outlets and social constructs surrounding us that the world is an unsafe place and that we have to use the weapons of our will power and fear to get our rightful share and protect those we care about. We are taught to believe in scarcity over abundance, competition over unity, logic over imagination, and immediate gratification over commitment. These beliefs undermine our true potential and leave us feeling spiritually vacuous. They leave no room for the boundless love and gratitude that is deep within each of us for the world we share and the incredible offerings we can give. Simply put, these beliefs put out the flame of our life purpose. You'll learn all about this in the fourth strategy on seeing your obstacles to purpose.

Wow, this all sounds kind of heavy.

Is there any good news?

So now that we have identified this rather deep problem that most people in our society are faced with, I bet you're ready to hear something uplifting. Identifying the problem is certainly a good start. We have to be aware of how we got to where we are and we have to be able to understand our problems in the right context. But this really is just the beginning. For each of us, a rather substantial part of our life purpose involves freeing ourselves from whatever trauma we have experienced. It is about identifying a place inside of us that has never been damaged, limited, deceived, or traumatized. For many of us, identifying with this place is a revolutionary beginning to a new life because it simply hasn't been done before. This inner refuge is not something that you have to believe in per se. It is more the direct experience of your actual nature. It is what naturally surfaces when we remove all of the harmful conditioning that has been piled upon it. Admittedly, this may sound like a leap of faith from where you currently are, but the rest of these strategies have been designed to give you a firsthand experience of the wisdom that you have been innately endowed with.

THE GOOD NEWS IS TWOFOLD

1 You have this awake, wise, and joyful essence within yourself. *Yes, you!* It has not been impacted by the society you live in, the way your parents raised you, **how long** you have been off track, or any bad things that have hap**pened** to you in your life. It is still intact, ready to be awakened and expressed to the world.

2 You can contact this essence at any moment! It is always available to you and always has been. It doesn't matter how old, young, pained, jaded, cynical, stuck, or stressed out you are. You can literally drop all of the suffering, mediocrity, or hardship you have endured right

now and start living from this place of purpose. Even if you are 70 years old and have been stuck in a lifelong pattern of pain or dissatisfaction, you have a right to experience this source of well-being this very moment. This essence is always there. Your life purpose is the active manifestation of this essence into the world. The steps laid out in these strategies will show you exactly how to start living in this way starting right now.

When we engage with our purpose, we finally see that we were never meant to endure prolonged struggle or suffering. We were never meant to feel uninspired, discouraged, hopeless, bored, or frustrated by our lives. We were never meant to resign ourselves to a life that is just okay. We begin to see that we deserve so much more than this and that we have a sacred duty to help others realize their right to a life of freedom and well-being. We are meant to be free and to help others do the same. As you will discover through working with these strategies, the process of uncovering your purpose and claiming your right to freedom and fulfillment begins right here, right now.

But how? How do I find this place within myself?
How do I change? How do I open myself up to all of this?

Before we move on, it is vital that we address the question that seems to hold so many of us back: *How?*

It's easy to get stuck in how. In fact, moving through the potential block of "but how?" is an important part of evolving on your path toward purpose. Ultimately the question of how has no relevance. The real question is not how, but why? Why should I change? Why should I live with purpose? Why open my heart? When your why crystallizes into a strong enough desire for a life of freedom and purpose, the how automatically falls into place.

The steps outlined in the next several strategies are as close as we can come to answering the question how. But unless your desire for freedom is strong enough, you can easily use even this information to further confuse yourself, create more obstacles, and postpone what matters most to you. Whenever you notice that you have become stuck in how, consider it a red flag that you need to return to your mission to live with purpose and your intention for freedom. That desire will navigate you through all of the confusion that can arise in relation to how you actually do it.

EXERCISE

For each writing exercise mentioned in this book, it is most effective to write in a stream of consciousness way. No editing, judging, or critiquing yourself as you put pen to paper. Just let it flow. Don't allow yourself to stop writing. Keep the pen moving. First thought, best thought.

1 Spend some time every day learning about the spiritual traditions of the world and how they have viewed life purpose. What you will discover is that every prophet and revered spiritual figure (Buddha, Jesus, Mohammed, and others) has asserted the truth that every being has a sacred purpose. Read spiritually uplifting books by those who are expressing their purpose through their writing so it can continue to inspire and teach you after you make it through all of these strategies.

Now, let's move on to the next strategy that will unlock your purpose and help you achieve optimum wellness. Each of these strategies can be applied to every aspect of your life that is lacking purpose. The basic foundation is always the same. As you begin to work with these steps, remember that this is a practice that will likely feel awkward as you transition into a new way of being.

Don't worry if you feel like you're doing it wrong or you have moments when you forget to focus. That will likely happen. Remember, it is a practice. All that is required is that you bring a quality of wholeheartedness to these steps and that you approach them with as much sincerity and earnestness as you can find within yourself. And don't forget to come back to the "beginner's mind" we talked about earlier. If you do that, you are doing your best. That is all that is required to unlock the door to your life purpose.

To Know Your Sacred Purpose
First Focus on Being, Then on Doing

If you cannot find the truth right where you are,
where else do you expect to find it?

— D o g e n   Z e n j i

In our modern world, we are typically led to believe that the solutions to our problems exist outside of ourselves. As a by-product of this belief, we feel that we must stay in a perpetual state of motion in order to perceive ourselves as successful so we can feel better. If we are always doing something, which brings us closer to the solutions "out there," then we feel like we're holding up our end of the bargain. We believe that we're avoiding one of the greatest societal prejudices of all: being a lazy and unproductive person. If we do slow down, we often feel guilty or restless.

The problem is that we often try to discover our life purpose under the premise that it also is outside of us and that we need to achieve, learn, and do a lot in order to actualize it. We feel that who we are right now is incomplete and that when we finally discover our purpose, we will get to be whole at last. This sets us up for a fundamental quandary: When we operate under the assumption that we are incomplete right now and that we need something outside of us or in some future time in order to feel better, we will forever be denied access to the state of total wellness and joy that we are seeking.

First and foremost, life purpose is a state of being. This means that the primary purpose for every human being is about anchoring their full sense of awareness to this very moment. Whatever we "do" to achieve fulfillment and meaning in the world must be grounded by our willingness to preside fully in present moment reality.

All too often, we use our outer accomplishments and roles as a way to fill the spiritual void we feel from not being fully awake to this moment. We compensate for our resistance to the present moment by constantly doing something, whether it's exercise, working, worrying, or thinking about what we're going to do or what we have done. This is our way to ensure our survival and feel in control. When we are constantly doing, we cannot see the gap in our moment-to-moment reality, the silence and space that always underlies our life experience.

Our outer accomplishments and roles are always subject to change. They will one day come to an end. There is nothing permanent or stable we can hold on to and say, "This is who I am. This is my purpose." They are always based on the conditions of the moment. If your life purpose is to be a violinist, but then you get crippling arthritis and can no longer play, what is your purpose then?

This is why the state of your being is always the ultimate source of your purpose. Anything that happens on the outside is subject to change. When we become overly identified with our accomplishments, we will inevitably experience disappointment when our conventional roles fade away due to the universal law of impermanence, which is that everything that arises will eventually pass away.

Your primary job as a human being is to break free of the confines of your self-imposed limitations. This is not something that can you "do" or "accomplish"; rather, it is a fundamental shift in the way you perceive yourself and your role in the universe.

When you focus on being, you put your entire faculty of awareness into this very moment. You see through the illusion of time. You keep returning to the innate sense of completion within yourself right now. In an ultimate sense, there is nothing missing. When you see your primary purpose in life as practicing the recognition of your inherent perfection as a human being, your daily life will take on an entirely new dimension of freedom and wellness. You will feel that your full sense of Self has come alive and is fully inhabiting this moment.

When you see your purpose in this way, your outer work takes on a new meaning. You are now able to bring a much lighter, more energized quality to your "doing" that is infused with Spirit and enthusiasm. You are able to get "in the zone," as you are not attached to the outcome of your activities because you already feel fundamentally okay with yourself. Many of us assume that focusing on the perfection of Being would make us feel lazy, like we wouldn't have a desire to accomplish anything. Interestingly, just the opposite is true. When we practice being fully plugged into the completion of this moment, our consciousness goes through a process of expansion that generates a tremendous amount of compassion for the outside world. Instead of doing a lot to make ourselves feel better or more accomplished, we use our time and energy to help others. We feel an earnest desire to use our life as a vehicle for service.

We will talk about generosity as a gateway to infinite freedom in another strategy. For now, your job is to take a radical departure from any and all conditioning that has been pumped into you that suggests that the answers are outside of you in some future time. Let go of the misconception that you need to perpetually remain in "doing" mode in order to feel fulfilled and well. Consider the possibility that just the opposite is true. Much of your life can be devoted to just being, to cultivating a heightened state of consciousness that will make your doing so much more potent and helpful. Be honest with yourself and assess to what degree you have chosen a lifestyle and mindset where time, which doesn't actually exist, is perceived as a scarcity—especially if you are someone who tends to use "I don't have time" as a daily mantra.

Some of us will say that we actually thrive in a state of constant doing. When we get rewarded for our constant motion in the form of money or various accolades, we convince ourselves that we are thriving. But really, we are just stuck in a game of avoiding ourselves. The problem is that when we are fixated on doing, then we are just running on adrenaline. We have a daily to-do list that is a mile long. We stay in perpetual motion, always filling our plate with activities and responsibilities. We become addicted to the speed of our daily life, which burns our internal resources and sets the state for premature aging and stress-related disorders. When this occurs, we will miss out on the vast reservoir of wellness that lies at the core of our Being. The adrenaline junkie lifestyle can only offer us a miniscule fraction of the fulfillment and joy that comes from focusing on this reservoir.

Keeping it practical, what this really boils down to is being able to constantly recognize the state of your consciousness as being the most primary influence on the quality and circumstances of your life. In order to change your circumstances, you must change your consciousness. Your level of spiritual awareness, which is determined by how much you have cleared the obstacles to purpose, will always provide the most direct input into the outer world that keeps showing up in your life.

MOVING AWAY FROM THE MODERN MINDSET

When your primary focus is on being instead of doing, you are aligning with the laws of the universe. You are setting the stage to be a vessel of abundance and balance rather than will power and fear. You are going against the grain of a collective modern mindset that says, "Get out there, work your butt off, and get your fair share." This modern mindset is steeped in scarcity consciousness, which asserts that there simply isn't enough for everyone, so every person has to use whatever means necessary to assure their personal gain. For the sake of clarifying the modern mindset that most of us have been deeply influenced by, let's take a quick look at the main features of the scarcity mindset, then we'll spend nearly the entire remainder of this book strategizing solutions for getting you to a place of purpose:

- ◎ Being a victim
- ◎ Looking outside of yourself for the answers
- ◎ Placing blame on others when things don't work out
- ◎ Resigning yourself to mediocre circumstances because it feels safe
- ◎ Feeling separate from the infinite forces of the universe
- ◎ Feeling separate from other people
- ◎ Postponing what really matters to you
- ◎ Putting money before anything else

The essence of this strategy is that we need to maintain a continual focus on our inner reality in order for our outer reality to flow as we want it to. Our inner world is always the most important influence. As a corollary, the present moment is always the only entry point we have to life purpose.

Any questions?

I have tried in the past to visualize and feel what I want , but it never seems to work. I'm left feeling like I just don't get how to use my awareness in the right way. What am I doing wrong?

Ironically, trying to visualize what you want can be another thing that you "do" in the attempt to be happier, more successful, or wealthy. When we focus on being, the first step is always to give up any agenda or expectation we have about life being different than it is in this moment. The whole point is that we actually are complete in this moment—not as a contrived feeling or mental image. As you'll learn through the following strategies, there is certainly an authentic way to use the power of the mind to change your outer life. We have to be careful with this power, though, because it can easily pull us in the direction of disappointment or confusion. In the situation described here, the problem is likely that you aren't clear enough about who you really are and what you really want, which weakens the power of visualization.

What you will learn in the following strategies will offer you a powerful blueprint for making this shift into your inner being so that you can indeed create an outer reality that exemplifies your purpose. In particular, the ninth strategy will teach you a variety of practical steps you can take to ground all of this material into your daily life.

Let's move on to the next strategy. Now that it is clear that the present moment is your entry point into a life of purpose, we need to discuss how you can actually invoke purpose into your life using your faculties of awareness and intention.

Put Your Purpose First

Often people attempt to live their lives backwards;
they try to have more things, or more money, in order
to do more of what they want, so they will be happier.
The way it actually works is the reverse. You must first
be who you really are, then do what you need to do, in
order to have what you want.

— M a r g a r e t   Y o u n g

Okay, in the first two strategies we covered a lot of ground. We clarified that each of us has a sacred purpose for being here and that it's vital to our health, success, and well-being to understand this. We also suggested that life purpose begins with the state of your being, your consciousness in this moment, and then extends out to what you do.

The next series of strategies are dedicated to helping you discover your purpose and how to effectively handle some of the potential obstacles that may arise as you embark on this process. Make sure you listen very closely to this strategy, for if you allow this message in fully, you are giving yourself a most special gift.

THE POWER IN ASKING FOR PURPOSE

Starting right now, wherever you are at in your life, the first step you need to take in order to activate your life purpose is declaring to yourself that you are ready to feel, receive, and uncover it. Start asking for this all of the time. In every action you initiate, word you speak, and encounter you have, set an intention that you are indeed ready to engage with your purpose. What you are essentially saying is that you are ready to take responsibility for yourself and your life. Starting right now, you are ready to know that your life has a sacred purpose. You are ready to make an imprint on the world, to show up and be accountable for who you are and what you have to offer. You are done with ignoring your purpose or pretending that it doesn't exist. You no longer feel compelled to live your life in a way that obscures your purpose. Affirm that you are ready to stop the momentum of whatever is blocking it from surfacing.

At this point, the exact form that your purpose will take is not important. Please keep that in mind. Even if you have no idea what you are meant to be doing with your life, that is okay. By asking for your purpose to arise, you are first and foremost asking your Spirit to inhabit you fully and to guide you in your life. You are initiating a conversation with the deepest essence of who you are. You are invoking the presence of your purpose-based Self by asking it to surface.

By asking for purpose all of the time, you are changing your relationship with the world from the inside out. Instead of waiting for some sort of external confirmation to show you what you are supposed to do, you start by making a fundamental shift in your inner reality. Since most of us have been taught to look for the answers "out there," this can be a radically new way of relating to life. We are initiating the process of change through our own heart and mind regardless of what is showing up in our outer life.

WHAT MAKES US FINALLY READY TO ASK FOR PURPOSE?

How do we come to this place of declaring the immediate importance of our purpose? Well, for many of us, we have to literally exhaust every other option. We have to completely see through the way we have been living. We have to expose our tendencies to avoid ourselves and to stay in a state of distraction. Many of us come to this place of declaring a readiness to receive purpose when we just can't take any more struggle and pain. We are finally willing to consider another way of living, even it means relinquishing our control over life and what is familiar or comfortable to us.

Some of us describe it as exhaustion or desperation that brings us to a place of purpose. Ironically, when we feel the worst, when we have sunk into a deep place of hopelessness or pain, we are often much closer to our purpose than we have ever been. Why? Because we're finally willing to give up what is known to us. We are willing to consider a reality beyond what we have validated up to this point. This is why issues around life purpose tend to become more magnified around events such as the death of a loved one, divorce, illness, or a financial crisis. If we choose, these circumstances can wake us up to a new understanding of ourselves and our role in the universe. The key point is to be able to use these events as opportunities to free yourself from limiting beliefs rather than as further evidence to reinforce what you already believe to be true. By doing this, you can learn the lesson you need to learn and liberate that painful event rather than prolong it.

Say you get struck with financial crisis and have to go bankrupt. When you hear news like this, what does it mean to put your life purpose first? Well, the habitual or normal way of going about it would be to use this news to support what you already think about yourself and life in general. For some of us, a voice would creep in that declares, "I have always known that life is unfair. No matter how hard I try, things always end up this way." For others, such an experience would validate our feelings of unworthiness. We would use this as yet another source of self-negation. These beliefs would keep us in alignment with continued financial hardship. No matter how hard we try to change it, we find that we are always on the brink of financial disaster.

When you are ready to respond with purpose, you'll be willing to drop any and all storylines about this development that support feelings of separation, victimization, or how you have been wronged. Instead, you'll be ready to take a fresh look at the situation and see it with new eyes. While you won't want to go bankrupt, you'll be willing to perceive it as a teacher that can open you up to many life lessons that you have likely missed out on. You'll use it as a way to open your heart fully, face the impermanence of being human, and connect more deeply with others. It may fill you with an entirely new sense of meaning in your life. This is why many people have said that financial crisis has been the best wake-up call they could have asked for. It was a catalyst that opened them up to a more sacred relationship with life. They chose to find themselves in the midst of (often extreme) hardship. The person who finds their way out of this situation to a more purposeful life has made a fundamental shift in their inner reality; they have cleared the inner block that has kept them attracting the same painful circumstances over and over.

OUR INTERPRETATIONS OF LIFE
EITHER OPEN US TO OR BLOCK US FROM PURPOSE

Every life event gives us the opportunity to shed any beliefs or perceptions that weigh us down. It is commonplace, however, to use the circumstances of life to build more armoring around our hearts and to strengthen our convictions about who we are and how life is. From the time we are little, we are inundated with the beliefs of others regarding how to live, act, and be in the world. As children, we are like absorbent little sponges that soak up the deeply impactful messages of the numerous forces that surround us. Eventually, as our little minds develop the ability to think and conceive, we take all that we have absorbed and impart our own subjective meaning to our life experience.

This sets the process in motion of forgetting who we really are. Our spontaneous and flowing connection with the universe is replaced by all of the "stuff" that has been pumped into us from the outside world. As such, we begin to distort reality into the understanding that it is life itself that is causing us to suffer rather than our perceptions of it. Based on the cultural worldview that we are born into, our beliefs become coping mechanisms to protect us against the alienation we feel in relation to the universe. Since we now perceive ourselves as separate from the infinite universe from which we came, we lose touch with the wisdom and power that has always been our nature. We turn to the outside world for validation.

The delicate developmental stages of early childhood create a profound imprint that often rules us well into adulthood, possibly forever. The problem is that most of us have never learned the importance of honestly assessing our beliefs and values and truly determining if they are enslaving or freeing us. The older we become, the more sophisticated our defenses against such an honest assessment become. Without a willingness to plunge heart-first into our long-held beliefs, it is highly likely that we will live out our days on autopilot pretty much acting out the examples that were set for us at a very young age. The phase of development from birth to age five is often so impressionable that we never really evolve out of it. Unless we proactively challenge it, we take what we were taught during this time and continually reenact it into the world for as long as we live. This inevitably leads to a life of imbalance, struggle, mediocrity, and resistance. This is because the worldview that is formed during this time is, as mentioned, based on a very narrow interpretation of life that clamps us down to a tenuous set of conditions that serve as our self-identity.

This third strategy, being willing to put your purpose first, is when you finally and fully declare that you choose, more than anything else in your life, to free yourself from limiting beliefs, habits, and addictions so that you can begin to have a direct relationship with your purpose: who you really are and why you're really here. You absolutely can do this right now. If you're like many people, however, you have created a lifestyle that is steering you in the opposite direction from making this kind of declaration. The momentum you have established runs contrary to the fulfillment of this crucial step. Indeed, taking this step can be a radical departure from the life you currently have. That's okay. Creating purpose is not meant to be hard. It is always accessible, no matter how far removed it seems from your current lifestyle. This will become more apparent after reading the next several strategies.

THE CHOOSING FACULTY

At any moment you have a choice, that either moves you closer to your Spirit or further away from it.

—Thich Nhat Hanh

In order to put your purpose first, you have to realize that you have a choice in each moment to contract or expand. You can choose to go up or down, evolve or sink. If you are in a spiritually receptive place, the realization that you choose your relationship with life will be deeply empowering. If, however, you are still more invested in distracting yourself from your purpose, then you will ignore, rationalize against, or violently resist the idea that you have free will to choose how you relate to life.

There are indeed many forces at work in our modern world that are masterful at obscuring our power to choose. They will do anything to prevent us from seeing how much power we have in how we think, act, and feel. When we buy into this, we will be convinced that we are powerless to change our outer circumstances. Putting your purpose first means that you are willing to look at every single feeling you have and situation you're in as open-ended. When you feel depressed, you choose to relate to yourself with compassion. You decide to get some exercise and eat a nourishing meal. When you are stressed out, you choose to settle your mind and body by breathing deeply so you can consciously cut through the frenzied momentum of your thoughts. When you compulsively reach for the gallon of ice cream, you choose to stop, breathe, and observe your motivations. When you are struggling through an argument with your spouse, you choose to let go of the need to be right and you soften. When you realize that your job has become a dead end, you choose to create an exit strategy and an action plan for a much more rewarding career.

CASE STUDY ~~ JILL ~~

Jill came to my acupuncture practice with a 15-year history of persistent migraine headaches. She was a successful lawyer who worked very hard and endured a high degree of stress. At first, Jill came to see me to manage her headaches, so she could continue to work hard without having to be bothered by crippling pain.

The problem was that Jill did not like her job. In fact, as her awareness grew, she had less tolerance for the daily grind that wreaked so much havoc on her mind and body. She realized that her decision to become a lawyer was largely based on a belief system that she had to be constantly pushing herself or else she was lazy and useless and would end up in poverty.

After several acupuncture sessions, it was clear that Jill was learning how to listen to her body's symptoms. She chose to pay attention to the warning signs her body was giving her. As a result, she began to consider what her deeper purpose was based on the increased awareness she was developing. She decided to put her purpose first. Jill made it a daily practice to contemplate what would most ideally match her unique gifts and what would make her feel the healthiest and happiest.

After mustering up a great deal of courage to see through her belief that she had to stay constantly busy, Jill came to the conclusion that her purpose was to enjoy a prolonged period of rest. She decided that the most useful thing she could do with her life was to do very little and to focus

continued

on her inner being. Jill made the wise and brave decision to act on this realization by quitting her job and taking a prolonged sabbatical to restructure her life. Not surprisingly, the migraines that had plagued her for 15 years ceased almost instantly.

Jill was ready to put her purpose first. She realized that this mattered more than anything else. She clearly saw how any other course she would have taken in her life would have led to deteriorating health, more pain, and higher stress. By putting her purpose first, Jill tapped into a level of wellness in her life that she could never have previously imagined..

In every moment, you have a choice. Realizing this is one of the secret keys to unlocking your purpose. Why? Because knowing that you have a choice means that you will never be a victim to life again. You will never again be tempted to perceive outer circumstances or your emotional states as stronger than you are. You will realize that in each moment you possess an innate resource of wisdom and awareness that can help you choose the highest state of consciousness and best course of action.

Even if you've been enslaved by crippling depression or horrible acts of injustice, you can choose to put your purpose first right now. What this means is that you are choosing to use these sources of suffering as fuel for your evolutionary fire. You are choosing to use them as a bridge that more deeply connects you with others. Instead of identifying with past pains and traumas as who you are, you are choosing to identify with the vast space of your nature that has not and cannot ever feel wounded or damaged.

In the next strategy, we'll take a clear look at the main obstacles we face in choosing our purpose. For now, just make it a practice to empower yourself in this way. Activating this choosing faculty is entirely based on your willingness to do so. While it may sound like a given that every one of us would be willing to see that we can choose a life of freedom, it is not quite that simple. This kind of willingness connotes full accountability to our life. We have to be willing to acknowledge the profound impact that our presence has on other people, life forms, and the universe as a whole.

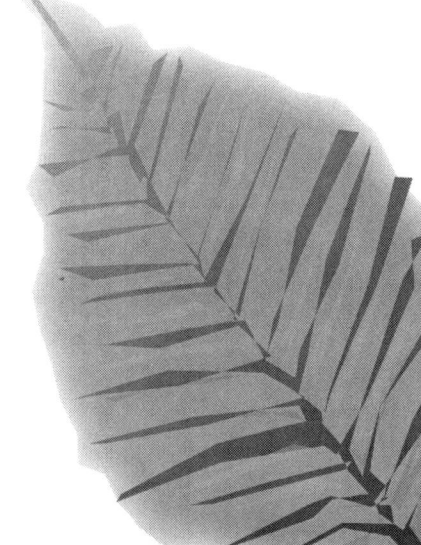

This kind of willingness suggests an inner knowing that we can't get away with anything. Every intention, thought, and action makes an imprint on this world. We reap what we sow in every moment. There is no escape from this.

In this sense, we shoulder the responsibility of being a light unto this world and stepping into our immense personal power. While this may sound like an immense undertaking right now, it's also important to know that it is the basis of ultimate freedom, creative joy, and optimum wellness.

WHETHER YOU FEEL READY OR NOT, TAKE THIS FIRST STEP RIGHT NOW

This third strategy, declaring the importance of our purpose, becomes a reality when we can embrace our personal power and invoke a force from deep within our Being that knows what it's here to do. When we make this declaration, we are confirming the fact that we are absolutely done with deception, distractions, addictions, or anything else that is taking us away from ourselves.

At the beginning of this chapter, we highlighted the fact that many of us don't experience our life purpose until the universe presents us with a rather stark call to awaken, often in the form of illness, major life transition, divorce, or the loss of a loved one. While it is certainly better to tap into our purpose through hardship than never to do it at all, it's crucial to our well-being to utilize the enormous opportunity in this very moment to declare the importance of our purpose. We don't have to wait for a really strong message from the universe. We can actually choose to embark on the path of purpose right now, in this very moment. Most of us, however, are just too comfortable in the life we have created to take this seriously. We just don't have a sincere and burning desire to put this issue at the top of our priority list. How could this possibly be?

Well, the path of purpose isn't necessarily one that validates our need for security or comfort. In fact, part of the process of invoking purpose involves willingly calling out all our demons, deceptions, and vices with the intention of saying to them, "I am no longer attached to you." This can be an emotionally intense and cathartic process that would not be described as enjoyable in the conventional sense, but is often a deeply exhilarating and empowering experience in the spiritual sense. Declaring the importance of purpose means that we are willing to expose our fear, vulnerability, and layers of addiction, narcissism, and/or self-deception. While the potential fruits of doing this work on ourselves are indeed glorious beyond comprehension, there is still a part of each of us that obstinately affirms, "I am fine as I am, thank you very much."

THERE IS A PART OF YOU THAT
WILL NEVER BE READY

We have to see that there is a part of us that will never be ready to take this first step. It is the force within us that convinces us that we have time to put off what is most important in life. It believes in tomorrow much, much more than it does in this very moment. It keeps us locked in a state of negotiating with ourselves to keep participating in thoughts, emotions, and actions that are misaligned with our essential nature and purpose. It gives us countless "solid" excuses as to why we need to continue on in a job that we dislike, a marriage that is dying, or an addiction that undermines our life force. It keeps us bound up in a state of "getting ready" to make the changes we need to make for our own well-being, but somehow never get around to making because some condition or another isn't right for us to finally do it.

The greatest danger we face is allowing this part of ourselves to run the show day after day, year after year. We do our best to try to understand this part of ourselves, make it feel better, negotiate with it, and comfort it, which ultimately feeds this part of us and makes it stronger. We have to be willing to see that this part of us will never, ever change and has no interest in doing so. It is hell-bent on keeping things as they are, even if that means that we settle for a life that is far below our potential. For the rest of the strategies, we will refer to this place as the "small self." The good news is that this small self has never been anything but an illusion. It is in no way the real you, no matter how convincing it may be.

It is nothing more than the accumulation of what you have been taught about who you are and how life is. Because of this, it can be dissolved at anytime, but only when you decide that you are ready to dissolve it. The small self will do whatever it possibly can to hold on to its territory and protect what is familiar. For all of us, it is an incredibly seductive force that deceives us into keeping our focus on it. When we focus on it, we feed it and it grows. The rest of the strategies you will learn will show you as clearly as possible how to stop feeding this fear-based illusion that is never ready to change. Starting with the next strategy, you will begin to expose the small self, to see it as separate from you. In order to activate the Purpose Principle in your life, you have to disentangle yourself from identifying with this conditioned and false shadow that lurks beneath your conscious awareness.

THERE IS A PART OF YOU THAT IS 100% READY FOR PURPOSE, RIGHT HERE AND NOW

Putting our purpose first means that we are ready to come from a new place entirely, one that has absolutely nothing to do with this fear-based, contracted place that only wants what is familiar. This new place has actually always been within you. It's just that you may have never really noticed it since your focus has likely been on the place that's not ready for change.

Making contact with and expressing your purpose can only happen in this very moment. Time is, after all, an illusion. If we think that we will get to our purpose at some point in the future when we are smarter, thinner, in a better relationship, or a better job, or when we no longer dislike ourselves, we are missing the power for change in this very moment. Freedom is available to you right now. It is not about some external condition that has to be met in order to be free. It is an intrinsic state, a spiritual quality that is the essence of your true nature as a human being.

Freedom comes from within, not at some point in the unforeseeable future, not tomorrow, but right now. If you can declare the importance of activating your purpose to experience a level of freedom and fulfillment in this very moment, the prognosis is very good. If you feel like your purpose can only come when some outer condition is met, watch out. You are in danger of spending the rest of your life stuck in a state of waiting to be ready for "the real deal." Now is all you have. Drop whatever voice within you is saying you have time. That is the most danger-ous way to live—pretending like you can get to all of this spiritual stuff later.

You could say that this purpose-based place within yourself is the real you, but this isn't really true either. Why? Because this place within yourself is way beyond the concept of "you" or "I." It cannot really be defined or captured by concepts at all. This may seem a bit hard to grasp at this point, which is just fine. No need to worry about that. Your job is simply to start setting a strong intention that you are ready to live with purpose, whatever that is. You are ready to stop distracting yourself from this sacred responsibility you have to live your best life. You are inviting in a new level of reality that may be much more powerful and vast than the one you are currently immersed in. If you can start with that, then you are in the place you need to be. Just keep working with each strategy without trying to force any of it.

At this point, stop reading. Do not move on to the next paragraph until you can honestly say that your purpose matters more to you than anything else. Affirm that you are ready to access this sacred treasure, even if it means relinquishing cherished beliefs, addictions, and relationships. If you are ready (and , once again, there is no real reason why you're not), you will be able to relate to yourself in an entirely new way, one that you most likely were never taught growing up, but that is the most powerful and genuine basis of true freedom in your life.

Any questions about our third srategy?

I have worked very hard to get to where I am in my life, but I am still not very happy. I would hate to feel like all of my effort to be successful has been for naught. I am afraid, however, that I haven't really put my purpose first based on the way it is being described here. What should I do?

When you put your purpose first, you have an opportunity to see that everything you have created up to this point in your life can be used to enhance and fuel what really matters to you. In this sense, there is no such thing as a mistake or a failure. All that you have is now. Regardless of your past, how you relate with this moment is all that matters.

It is usually not the case that we have been 100% alienated from our purpose in the major life decisions we have made up to this point. Certain pieces have been a fit, but certain others have not. For instance, some people decide that, after years of medical school, they really don't want to be a doctor after all. In that realization, they have a choice: to utilize all of the knowledge and experience they have gained to serve a different objective, or to lambaste themselves with judgment for what a horrible waste of time, money, and energy their schooling has been. Most likely, there is a wealth of benefit that they can take from their training and apply to whatever it is that provides them with more fulfillment at that point. People do this all the time.

We have already used the example of realizing that you want out of a failing marriage that you probably should have left 20 years ago. Rather than judging yourself for wasting all that time (which will only waste more time), putting your purpose first means that you will take action NOW, even if you realize it's 20 years overdue. By doing this, you will still have the opportunity to learn the lesson you needed to learn from that marriage so that you don't repeat the same mistake and so that you can help others to avoid making similar mistakes.

This same principle applies to anything in life that we have worked hard at but is no longer serving us in the right way. It is far better to cut your ties and follow your authentic calling (for a new job, marriage, or any other major life choice) than it is to resign yourself to what you have simply because it seems a waste to leave it based on how much of your life you have given to it. Whatever pain or resistance you were experiencing in the situation you need to leave can be seen as a lesson on getting closer to the life you really want. In this sense, it is only a waste of time if you prolong the truth and stick with it out of fear or obligation.

I think I want to put my purpose first, but I'm not really sure. How do I know?

If you're not sure, then you're not ready. You see, the small self LOVES confusion; it feeds off it. When we're stuck in "I'm not sure" and "but how?", the small self has effectively weakened the potency of our desire for purpose. The intensity and one-pointedness of your intention to live with purpose is the only solace you have against all of the distractions inside and outside of yourself that keep you at a distance from this. You're not ready because you still believe in these distractions more than you do your purpose. Until you exhaust this way of living, your purpose will remain suppressed within you. What are these distractions? The next strategy will make this clear.

This concept of the choosing faculty confuses me. If I suffer from really intense anxiety, how can I choose to not feel this way? How can I just choose to feel well?

It's not that you can choose to force the anxiety into nonexistence. That approach, which I'm sure you've tried, typically creates more of what you don't want, in this case anxiety. What you can do is choose to put your purpose first. You can choose to view the anxiety as a sacred teaching that can help you grow. You can choose to become very curious about the pattern of anxiety, why and when it shows up, and what makes it better. You can choose to depersonalize from the anxiety. You can choose to take responsibility for it and treat yourself with the utmost compassion. You can choose to hold the anxiety in an atmosphere of awareness and love.

Okay, I understand that, but my doctor told me that I have a biochemical disorder and that I should probably just stay on medication indefinitely because there's nothing else I can do, especially since my mother has struggled with the exact same issue. He told me that since it's a genetic issue, nothing can really help except medication.

The field of genetics has been premised upon the assertion that we are all born into this world with a concrete genetic code that will basically determine how we live. Much of Western medicine and philosophy is based on this understanding. The problem with this assertion is that it causes us to feel disempowered in the face of our struggles. How can we have a choosing faculty when our genes essentially predetermine our fate?

The emerging fields of epigenetics and neuroplasticity blow apart this outdated notion of genetic fate. Listen to what renowned epigeneticist Bruce Lipton says in his book, *The Biology of Belief: Unleashing the Power of Consciousness, Matter, and Miracles*:

> The science of epigenetics, which literally means "control above genetics," profoundly changes our understanding of how life is controlled. In the last decade, epigenetic research has established that DNA blueprints passed down through genes are not set in concrete at birth. Genes are not destiny! Environmental influences, including nutrition, stress and emotions, can modify those genes, without changing their basic blueprint. And those modifications, epigeneticists have discovered, can be passed on to future generations as surely as DNA blueprints are passed on via the Double Helix.[1]

Neuroplasticity is the science of the brain's capacity to change, which contradicts the long-cherished scientific dogma that our brain chemistry and neural patterning are fixed at birth. Listen to what Sharon Begley says about this new science in her book, *Train Your Mind, Change Your Brain*:

> The doctrine of the unchanging brain has had profound ramifications, none of them very optimistic. It led neurologists to assume that rehabilitation for adults who had suffered brain damage from a stroke was almost certainly a waste of time. It suggested that trying to alter the pathological brain wiring that underlies psychiatric diseases, such as obsessive-compulsive disorder (OCD) and depression, was a fool's errand. And it implied that other brain-based fixities, such as the happiness "set point" to which a person returns after the deepest tragedy or the greatest joy, are as unalterable as Earth's orbit.

But the dogma is wrong. In the last years of the twentieth century, a few iconoclastic neuroscientists challenged the paradigm that the adult brain cannot change and made discovery after discovery that, to the contrary, it retains stunning powers of neuroplasticity. The brain can indeed be rewired.[2]

The reason we are harping on these points is because it's crucial to understand the cultural dogma that you have been raised in that endlessly reinforces the belief that you don't have an innate power to change your life, and that your struggles and limitations are set in stone. This dogma runs through our religious and scientific institutions and has had a monumental effect on the way we are educated and conditioned. Simply put, it is impossible to experience the purpose-based wellness being discussed in this book if you buy into this dogma. The fields of epigenetics and neuroplasticity give us scientific proof that we can change and that we have the capacity to choose our destiny.

Of course, there are people who have some kind of organic brain damage and we have to be sensitive to their limitations. Even then, people in these situations almost always carry within them much more potential for transformation than is often realized.

The Purpose Principle does not exclude anyone. The whole thrust of healing your anxiety is based on recognizing the power of choice and then eventually transforming your current struggle into an opportunity to help others. What this conversation boils down to is the truth that you are not your anxiety; you are not your past; you are not your thoughts and feelings; you are not your genes, your body, or your biochemistry. Who you really are is much more powerful and vast than any of this. You can call this your Spirit, your higher Self, your purpose-based Self, or just pure awareness. It doesn't really matter. What does matter is that you choose to identify with this inner source starting right now.

When you declare that your purpose is more important than anything else, guess what tends to happen? You see with utmost clarity every inner and outer obstacle that is blocking you from actualizing your intention to live with purpose. This is such an important point to keep in mind if your expectation is that declaring the importance of purpose will automatically take you to an exalted state of freedom and wellness. You have to see what's blocking you first, and then you have to know how to relate to these obstacles. As you will see, making your obstacles conscious is an integral aspect of this foundation of the Purpose Principle. It is a necessary part of the path to ultimate freedom.

SEE Your Obstacles to Purpose

Obstacles will look large or small to you according to whether you are large or small.
—Orison Swett Marden

Welcome to the fourth strategy. If you have absorbed the previous strategy, you have made a profound shift by declaring the absolute importance and sacredness of your purpose. You have activated your choosing faculty so you can see that you have a choice in how you relate to each moment. Even if it feels somewhat subtle to do this at first, the more you declare for yourself that this is how you want to live, the quicker you will be able to actualize the life you really want.

WHILE THIS IS TRUE, WE NEED TO
ADD THE FOLLOWING CAVEAT

As a natural by-product of stating this intention, you will be put face to face with any and every dark, hidden, and deceptive part of yourself that simply does NOT want to go here. The small self wears many disguises, many of which will be revealed in this strategy. It is essential that we shed light on the internal and external forces that block us from a life of bound-less potential, joy, and freedom. When you state that your purpose comes first, you are inviting all of these blocks into your conscious awareness so that you can ultimately liberate them.

This is why life can initially seem harder when you ask for purpose. You are willingly exposing what has blocked you from being fully present to your life and activating your innate gifts, heartfelt aspirations, and limitless potential.

This is such an important point because it is so easy to steer away from our purpose if we have been led to believe that we should feel better when we decide to move toward it. For some people, this is the case. Life instantly becomes lighter, more expansive, and joyful. For many others, however, it can feel like the life we have known and the worldview we have cherished are unraveling before our very eyes.

It's helpful to know that this may not feel "good" in the conventional sense of the term. Many people describe it as a feeling of groundlessness, intense exhilaration, catharsis, or even a questioning of their basic sanity. These feelings are based on a stripping away of who we thought we were. When we invite our obstacles to surface with the intention of freeing them, we are essentially letting go of our conditioned self-image. We are no longer able to define ourselves based on our conditioned beliefs, emotions, or thoughts. Indeed, living with purpose is so often a process of being able to hang out in the unknown, in keeping the mystery of our own nature alive.

SUBCONSCIOUS HOLDING PATTERNS

A big part of asking for purpose is the process of allowing our subconscious holding patterns to become conscious. These are all of the forces, beliefs, and feelings we have about ourselves that block us from the life we really want. We will call them holding patterns throughout this book because they are literally what hold us back in life. They keep us spinning our wheels endlessly around the same perceptions, attitudes, actions, and results.

By putting our purpose first, we are inviting these holding patterns to our conscious awareness so we know what we are really working with. After all, every single one of us will say that we want happiness, prosperity, and peace in our lives. Who doesn't? But why do so many of us seem to be unable to access these wonderful qualities? It is because we are enslaved by subconscious obstacles that block us from what we desire. We may be telling ourselves that we want more money, success, and happiness, but our deeper subconscious belief system is based on internal forces that contradict these desires. An example would be the holding pattern of low self-worth, which continually reinforces the perception, "I don't really deserve what I want."

Making our subconscious holding patterns part of our conscious awareness can only happen when we have a one-pointed intention and willingness to see them as they are. We have to bring them into the daylight. Normally, they lurk around in the dark corners of our bodies and minds, setting us up for self-sabotage and struggle. While there are many techniques that have been created to make these subconscious holding patterns conscious (hypnosis, Emotional Freedom Technique, bodywork, and meditation to name a few), what is essential is that we have a true willingness to expose these dark recesses of our subconscious so that we can live in complete light. Without a genuine interest in doing this work on ourselves, there is no technique that can help us. For some people, all that is required is this *willingness*. Other people seem to need to utilize specific techniques such as these in addition to declaring the importance of their purpose. In this sense, every one of us has a different entry point into a life of pure honesty and authenticity.

WHY WE HAVE OBSTACLES TO PURPOSE

All of the blocks to purpose arise as a means of self-protection. To the extent that we have inner obstacles to purpose, we are basically trying to hold on to a sense of control in an eternal universe that is beyond our logical comprehension.

When we identify with our obstacles to purpose as who we are, then we become convinced that there is a solidity to life that we can control or rely on. Even if it is apparent that these obstacles are not at all empowering or helpful, we hold on to them because they are familiar and they make life feel more comfortable or predictable.

Let's examine these obstacles so we are clear about what needs to happen in order to open up this direct contact with our purpose. Once all of these obstacles are exposed, the fifth strategy will show you how to free yourself once and for all from anything that prevents your purpose from shining through. Our goal here is to simply gain an awareness of what blocks us from purpose. As you embark on this process, please keep in mind that it is not necessary to resurrect your entire past in order to create ultimate freedom. The most helpful intention you can have is to simply become aware of the forces within you that are preventing you from a life of purpose, balance, and fulfillment.

You do not need to dwell in these obstacles, identify with them, endlessly try to process through them, or spend a great deal of effort analyzing them. The goal is to simply see the content of the small self without judging or resisting it. Awareness itself heals. The next strategy will go much deeper into how to relate with the obstacles to purpose. For now, just keep this mantra alive within you: *Change happens now.* The small self is heavily invested in the idea that it takes a great deal of time and energy to heal and that it's really hard. It does this because it has absolutely no interest at all in making authentic change. You could say that the work involved in this strategy is being willing to see this part of yourself that actually feels validated by being stuck exactly where you are. You have to separate out your small self from who you really are if you are to live with purpose.

We want to be clear on this point so we don't just use this kind of self-inquiry as another way to identify with our storyline about how screwed up we are or how far away we are from our purpose. That is just more fuel for the small self.

Another mantra that perfectly summarizes the essence of this strategy:

See it and free it.

You can free these obstacles in a moment simply by realizing that they are not real, no matter how solid or difficult they may seem. They are a total illusion. More on this in the following strategies.

THE ONLY REAL OBSTACLE THERE IS

Every single obstacle you face on your path to purpose ultimately comes down to one main cause: Attachment. As we cover all of the following obstacles, it is essential that we clarify right up front here that every single state of mind we experience, every emotion, thought, and behavior, can be used as a means of bringing us closer to purpose as long as we aren't attached. This is why all of the upcoming obstacles are discussed in the context of attachment.

In the current New Age and spiritual approaches that are becoming so popular, there is a lot of talk about feeling good and positive thinking. Honestly though, when we aren't attached, the obstacles themselves can be just as or even more powerful forces to awaken purpose.

Nonattachment basically means that we don't personalize the content in our minds. We don't see negative or positive beliefs or states of mind as who we really are. When we can separate from the small self in this way, everything that the small self conjures up, whether it's fear, anger, or self-judgment, can be seen in the light of purposeful awareness. Every moment gives you the opportunity to awaken purpose. When your obstacles arise, this is the most powerful opportunity you have to glimpse your purpose, to go beyond the small self. After all, if it's not possible to do this when it's most difficult, when your mind is swimming in negative emotions or beliefs, then when can you do it? Life purpose is NOT about just feeling good. This is a very dangerous way to view the evolutionary process because you can easily be led to believe that discovering your purpose can only happen through positive feelings.

Instead, think of all the following obstacles as the most powerful opportunities you have to wake up and be free. If you allow your obstacles to habitually run you then yes, they are completely unhelpful. If, however, you can use them as a catalyst for your own spiritual and emotional development, then they are no longer obstacles per se. They are opportunities to awaken to a deeper level of being.

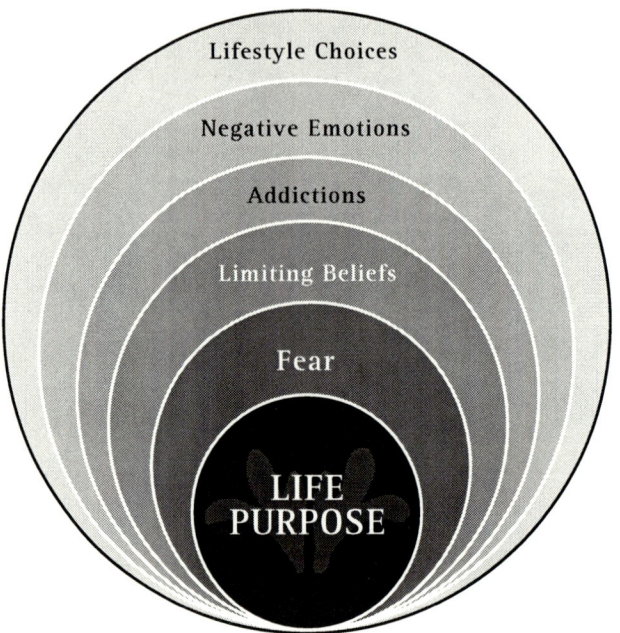

Lifestyle Choices

Negative Emotions

Addictions

Limiting Beliefs

Fear

LIFE PURPOSE

PEELING AWAY THE LAYERS TO OUR PURPOSE

The onion serves as one of the most helpful metaphors for understanding how we set up our lives with layers of obstacles to our purpose. Consider that at the center of the onion is our life purpose (refer to our second definition here: the identification and expression of our innate gifts, heartfelt aspirations, and limitless potential). The innermost barrier we have to this core of our being is attachment to fear. As we move to the next peel, we find the limiting beliefs that block us from our purpose and give us a false sense of control so that we don't have to face the fear. The next layer is attachment to negative emotions such as anger, jealousy, cynicism, or self-condemnation. The next layer is the habitual or addictive behavior we engage in on a regular basis. The outermost layer is the entire edifice of life that we have created or attracted to ourselves based on being separate from our innermost nature. This includes our lifestyle, job, marriage, friendships, diet, and other externalities. As we come to terms with the various imbalances of the life we have created, we have to be willing to cut through the outermost layer of our life experience, then our addictions, negative emotions, then to the next layer, our false beliefs, and then finally fear, until we can contact what we are best at and what we have to offer the world.

It's important to return to our first definition of purpose here as well: an awareness of present moment reality. If you are struggling with addictions, attachment to negative emotions, or fear, then your primary purpose should be always to bring awareness to these obstacles in this very moment and cut through their momentum (more on this in the next strategy). By putting your focus here, you are able to move closer to your innate gifts, heartfelt aspirations, and limitless potential.

FIRST OBSTACLE: Attachment to Fear— The Thickest Roadblock on the Path to Purpose

There seemed to be endless obstacles... it seemed that the root cause of all of them was fear.

—Joanna Field

When we consider dropping everything that is blocking our purpose from being actualized in this life, there is a force within each of us—the small self—that immediately wants to contract and cling to what is known. Even if we are thoroughly fed up with our mediocre plight in life, there is this obstinate thing within us that simply does not want to change. It is hell-bent on keeping things on autopilot and ensuring that our intention to take life deeper remains far away from reality. Inside each one of us, there is a small presence that is absolutely terrified of the unknown. It is only invested in what is known, even if the familiar has nothing to do with true fulfillment and freedom.

This small presence is the fuel for our self-sabotage, limiting beliefs, confusion, and frustration. It keeps us spinning our wheels only to end up in the same place over and over. If we define insanity as doing things the same way over and over and expecting a different result, then this is the force within us that makes us feel insane.

Fear. If you have grown up in the modern world, you are, to some degree, enslaved by it. Fear is the number one block that we face to our purpose. It is the prison guard that sits watch to make sure that we are staying locked up in ourselves.

When we honestly assess our blocks to purpose, fear is the obstacle that can easily fly beneath our radar screen. Many of us simply don't want to admit that we are afraid. It takes a sincere willingness to see all of the subtle shades of fear swirling around within us. Fear doesn't have to be an overpowering force that we feel only in relation to life-threatening events. In fact, most of the time, its workings are quite subtle.

All of us have been taught to give fear a lot of different names, like anger or depression, or to come up with different excuses as to why we are blocked. But underneath all of our reasons for not living the life that we want, there is fear. It is the layer of armoring that most vehemently denies our purpose. It is what causes us to contract around our purpose.

WHAT ARE WE MOST AFRAID OF?

1 **Death/impermanence:** We could say that all of our fear boils down to a basic aversion to change. We resist the fact that every single thing in this world is in a constant state of flux without any real solidity to it. Everything that is supposedly material is really just a vibrating mass of particles that are floating

in and out of existence. Even more so, our very identity has no solidity either. It is always changing, as our thoughts, feelings, opinions, and perceptions are constantly arising and passing away.

In order to launch our purpose, we have to be willing to let the small self die. In a very real sense, we can actually feel as if we are dying as we embark on the process of reinventing ourselves based on purpose. This is the level of fear that we need to go right into when we say that our purpose comes first. When we are willing to come face to face with the impermanence of this world, including ourselves, we then get to see how much power we carry within us as human beings. If we are not blocked by this fear of keeping our "self" going forever, then we tap into the limitlessness of our nature. There is no longer any "I" inside of us that feels pinned down to a limited understanding of what it is. Instead, we see that who we are is wide open. There are no boundaries. At this point, the small self will likely try to recoil again because it doesn't want to see the enormity of the universe and our human role within such unfathomable space. It hides in the light of this power that we all share. It doesn't want to take responsibility for this incredible life force that, when acknowledged and activated, can bring such immense benefit to others.

When we break through this level of fear, by owning our infinite power, then our purpose begins to fully awaken. In this sense, life purpose is a proclamation of freedom from this small self that is only interested in its own secure existence and does not want to see the enormous power that each of us shares simply by being alive in this universe. The final strategy on acknowledging death will explore this theme in depth.

2 **Failure:** Many of us turn our back on purpose because we are afraid of coming up short. We have been taught to see life through the dual lens

of success/failure. As you begin to work with the subsequent strategies, you will begin to see that there ultimately is no such thing as failure; there is only feedback. All that is happening is that the universe is giving us cues as to how on track we are in our pursuits. Rather than interpreting the cues we receive as a sign of our personal failure, we adapt to the changes we need to make based on the messages we're getting.

3 **Success:** If failure is one of the most common sources of fear, success is certainly right behind it. When we are taught from a young age that the power is outside of us and we should seek security at all costs, then we will fear the possibility of actualizing our infinite power and potential. We will cover our eyes when we are face to face with our inner light. Being successful means being accountable to life. The small self fears having to shoulder the responsibility that success of often brings.

4 **Giving up control:** We could say that our deepest fear is that we don't actually exist as the solid form of "I" that we have so cherished. In fact, nothing in the material world exists as we think it does. There is a veil of illusion to this whole phenomenon we call life. Our small self is freaked out about this. It is terrified that it has nothing to cling to as real and solid. There is no ground to stand on. When it senses this, it does whatever it can to cling to familiar reference points either through other people, food, beer, work, TV, or any other number of potential distractions. It holds on to confusion, ambivalence, and "I don't know how." These are all strategies that the small self uses quite effectively to maintain a false sense of control. When we cling to familiar reference points (even if they're not working for us), then we can assert for ourselves, "This is just who I am" and "This is just how life is."

When we are ready to live with purpose, we're ready to look at the fear we have without judgment. Even if at first your obstacles don't seem fear-based, keep peeling off the layers until you get to the deepest cause of your dissatisfaction or suffering. There is likely a fear of change and, even deeper, of the lack of certainty of who you are that is swirling around in your consciousness. The more honest we are with ourselves about this level of fear, the more quickly we will be able to create the life we really want. Going into this fear does not mean that it will never come up again. The more we commit to purpose, however, the weaker that suppressing force becomes. Instead of a paralyzing influence that shuts down your true passion and dreams, it becomes a little flicker that occasionally arises in the boundless space of your purpose-driven Self.

When we declare the importance of our purpose, we become willing to plunge headfirst into the things that scare us the most. Each of us has one core source of fear that keeps us feeling stuck. Our job is to start entering that fear so we can have a relationship with it. This does not mean that we indulge it or try to make it go away. It simply means that we are willing to investigate it. Interestingly, what we often discover is that our thoughts about what we fear the most are actually much more daunting than the direct experience of what we fear the most. When we enter our fear, we often find that there is something quite exhilarating within it that we have been missing out on in our lives. We find that there has been a lot of energy bound up within it. Perhaps what is most exhilarating is the realization that we are stronger than anything we fear.

Going into our fear is largely about giving up our false sense of control. In fact, we could list the need for control as its own obstacle to purpose, but since it is fueled by fear, we will mention it here. If you were raised in an environment where there was:

- Physical, emotional, or sexual abuse
- Financial instability
- Careless interactions between your parents
- A lack of structure, boundaries, or discipline
- Excessive structure or discipline

then you will very likely use your adult years to endlessly search for the control you never felt as a child. What we are ultimately searching for is a feeling of universal trust and safety that was sorely deficient in our childhood. This search can take on many different forms, such as:

- Trying to control your spouse by dictating what they do and who they relate with
- Trying to control your weight through compulsive eating, exercise, or habitual behaviors
- Trying to control your thoughts and emotions through spiritual exercises
- Being a perfectionist
- Being a type A go-getter who never takes a moment to breathe

Indeed, there are many ways that we try to control life. All of it is fueled by the lack of safety we feel in the universe. We were never taught or shown that the universe is an inherently friendly and benevolent place and that we belong in it. If this has been your experience as a child and adult, then the information in the next strategy will offer you a powerful way of releasing this kind of fear from your psyche.

SECOND OBSTACLE: Attachment to Our Beliefs—A Problematic Way of Establishing Our Identity in the World

If you're like most people in the modern world, you have absorbed a variety of beliefs about who you are and what life is about starting from the moment of your conception. Most of what you believe to be true was conditioned into you by the influences of your family. Your parents in particular served as the primary source of how you have come to understand the world. While most parents simply teach what they know in an effort to best protect their children, what often happens is that their actions serve as the deepest imprint on the beliefs that you form. Through their example, we identify with a certain way of being in the world. As we mature into adults, these beliefs tend to stick with us and become more sophisticated until we finally and fully challenge their validity and usefulness. First, we have to expose them, then we have to liberate them. That is the purpose of highlighting beliefs in the context of this and the following strategies.

Keep in mind that we attach to beliefs as who we are out of an instinctual need for self-protection; we were never shown or taught that we belong in the universe and that it is a safe, loving, and benevolent place for us to live. Harmful as they may be, these beliefs give us a false sense of control. They make us feel assured that we know who we are and how life works. Once again, what's important here is that you have a willingness to honestly examine your own beliefs that prevent you from expressing your purpose. Even if this feels awkward, uncomfortable, or frightening, doing this kind of work is a direct path to the life that you really want. This is not to say that you will have difficult feelings arise, as it can also be exhilarating to expose these beliefs with the intention of setting them free.

The end result of distorted beliefs is that they keep us in a perpetual state of ignoring our true nature. In a spiritual context, we can define ignorance not so much as an intellectual deficiency but as a habitual response to life in which we ignore the unlimited potential of each moment. This kind of ignorance is one of the most powerful obstacles to purpose; it keeps us in a state of delusion so that we aren't even aware of the ways we are inflicting harm on ourselves and others. It is like there is a cloud over our sense perceptions that keeps us in a chronic state of avoiding responsibility for our lives. This is completely fueled by what we believe to be true about ourselves and life in general.

Let's expose some of the most prevalent beliefs that many of us absorb at a very young age and how they serve to undermine our purpose. While there are many beliefs that can block us from purpose, these are some of the core ones that many of us carry around. As we expose the beliefs that undermine our potential, the rest of the strategies will focus on the path to clearing these blocks.

◈ **I am not good enough:** This one sentence is possibly the most widespread statement that we attach to that keeps us separate from purpose. When we don't feel good enough about who we are, we create a life of excessive giving in order to please others or we will need constant validation from others in order to feel okay. We end up people-pleasing, being really sweet and nice, and overly generous with our time, money, or energy. Or we feel stingy and have nothing to give because we are burdened by life. All of these tendencies naturally lead to resentment and burnout, as these habits are not aligned with who we really are. They cause us to leak energy and feel exhausted. We end up turning to food, sweets, or other indulgences in order to soak up a false source of energy. Many of us are taught that we are only accepted in the eyes of God if we harbor a notably self-deprecating stance with our lives. If we don't live this way, we feel guilty.

Not feeling good enough keeps us humble. We somehow feel validated in the process of never giving ourselves a full life. We can live year after year in a quiet state of dissatisfaction and pain, all the while maintaining an outward façade of generosity, kindness, and everything being okay.

The "not good enough" mentality is one of the most prevalent and profound blocks to purpose. When we are taught that we are incomplete beings who need to constantly strive for happiness and satisfaction, we become convinced as adults that our outer circumstances matter more than our inner world. We believe that our only hope for wholeness is found from something outside, whether it's in the form of a relationship, diet, job, exercise program, healer, or bank account. Instead of shifting our perception to recognize our inherent wholeness in this moment, we look to the outside world for solutions. For many of us, this creates a chronic cycle of trying to improve our lives only to end up in the same place of deficiency over and over. The next strategy will serve as the ultimate antidote to the "not good enough" mentality.

- **Life isn't fair**: With this belief, we can look at all of the injustices of the world and conclude that life isn't fair or even that God isn't fair. When this serves as our main belief, we tend to view life as a competition. We feel that we need to "get our share" because it's us against the world. We may even find ourselves in a competition with our spouse or people we love the most, always trying to stand our ground, defend what we know, and protect our coveted personal territory. If you find yourself saying with any kind of regularity, "This is just who I am" or "That's just how life is," then you are likely enslaved by this belief. At some point, this belief leads to resignation, frustration, and a black-and-white perspective on reality. Our achievements always feel at least subtly mired by the unfairness of life. We never take full joy and ownership of what we do and who we are. Instead, we stay in a constant state of hypervigilance, trying to create justice in a world where it doesn't seem to exist. The result is that we become extremely attached to being "right." This becomes more important than anything else, even love and life purpose.

❖ **Love isn't safe:** When we feel that love isn't safe, we become masters at avoiding genuine intimacy and a deeper connection with life. We spend our life keeping others at bay, creating games of distraction or drama that shield us from plunging headfirst into genuine intimacy. When we believe that love isn't safe, we can never really love ourselves. Therefore, we can never really know ourselves in our hearts, which keeps life superficial, like we're just skimming on the surface of this incredibly deep ocean that is our true reality. Love is the guiding force behind our life purpose. Ultimately, our purpose is always a vehicle for expressing our hearts and showering the world with love. This can only happen when we're willing to go into the heart of our lives and move through whatever insecurity or fear arises that keeps us at a distance from ourselves and others.

❖ **Nothing matters/I don't matter/Life has no value:** Many people in this day and age have grown up with an attitude of apathy or ambivalence. When this belief is running the show, there is no self-worth to be found. We feel empty and barren inside, as if we could die and nobody would notice or really even care. Often times, there is a spiritual quality that underlies this belief. We see that we came out of nowhere, we are now in this human body, and then at some undetermined point in the future, we will go back to nowhere. The whole thing just doesn't make much sense. Because of this, our hearts close and we feel as if we are already partly dead. We could take life or leave it. Many people caught in this belief are somehow able to make it through life, but they are acutely aware of a meaninglessness to the whole affair that severely hampers their actual potential.

- **Life is all about hard work:** Work ethic is indeed an important asset for a fulfilling and successful life. But it is certainly not the end-all be-all. In fact, if you believe that hard work is the main quality necessary to achieve your dreams, you are embarking on a path of exhaustion and painful repetition. You will find that you end up in the same place over and over again—in your work, your finances, your relationships. If this is the predominant belief, you will usually find that your health begins to plummet past the age of 40. Your body simply cannot keep up with your habitual drive and will power. It shuts down. With this belief, we assume that everything good in life requires hard work. The better it is, the harder we have to work to acquire it. We also believe that change is very hard. We have to "work" on ourselves in order to be a better person. As mentioned, our life purpose always has, at its core, a wonderful quality of effortlessness to it. Our hard work can actually be a deterrent to a life of flow and simplicity. Almost always, the underlying motivation behind our hard work is fear. When fear is motivating our actions, we will exhaust ourselves and feel that our potential is never even close to actualized, no matter how hard we try.

Here is a condensed overview of other predominant beliefs that are conditioned into us at a young age that block us from our purpose: [1]

- Love requires sacrifice.
- Suffering is noble.
- Change is hard.
- Worrying is a way of showing people you love them.

- Grieving for a lifetime means you really loved the person.
- Don't say something negative or be honest if it will hurt someone's feelings.
- A woman should never be outshined by her husband.
- The only real power is found outside of yourself.
- Marriage is forever, no matter what; people who divorce are failures

THIRD OBSTACLE: Attachment to Negative Emotions—Identifying with Struggle and Pain

When it comes to understanding and living out our purpose, there is room for the entire spectrum of human emotion, even anger, sadness, despair, grief, and worry. In fact, negative emotions can actually trigger a spontaneous awakening that brings us closer to a place of inner freedom. When we feel intense emotional pain, we have a sacred choice to make: contract even further or surrender to it. For now, just remember that negative emotions aren't really the problem; being attached to them is. When we express negative emotions out of habit, there is simply no room for life purpose.

The habitual expression of any negative emotion will only draw negative circumstances to us that make us feel justified in continuing to feel negative. The only way that negative emotion can persist is if we blame the outside world for the way we feel. This is a very effective way to never have to change the quality of our emotions. When we convince ourselves that the reason we are always angry is because of our job or our spouse, we will never take a look at the real source of our emotional discord.

What is the real source? Our negative emotions are always tied to the beliefs that we form to give us a sense of identity. For instance, if we feel that life is not fair, it is very likely that we will struggle with anger issues. If we believe that love isn't

safe, we will often struggle with sadness, withdrawal, or infidelity. If we feel like we
aren't enough, we will habitually worry and ruminate. If we believe that life doesn't
matter, then we will struggle with depression, apathy, and low self-worth. Negative
emotions arise directly out of our distorted beliefs.

In order to experience ultimate freedom in our work, finances, love life, and every
other area of life, we must release our attachment to negative emotions. The first
step is being willing to see what emotions we get seduced by or falsely identify
with. Remember, awareness is always the beginning reference point for freedom.

FOURTH OBSTACLE: Addictions—Clamping Ourselves off from the Spontaneity and Well-Being of Our Nature

In many Asian spiritual traditions, spontaneity is synonymous with health. When
we live spontaneously, we are free in each moment to proactively choose whatever
would best serve us and others. The opposite of spontaneity is addiction. This is
when our unconscious beliefs and negative emotions have become externalized
through habitual actions and coping mechanisms. You can think of addiction as a
more developed form of attachment that is born out of our identification with fear
and life-denying beliefs.

When we are run by false and limiting beliefs about who we are and why we're
here, we will inevitably form outer coping mechanisms that enable us to get
through life more comfortably. This is why our modern world struggles with such
a vast array of addictions. The root issue behind our addictive behavior is being
disconnected from our purpose. You could say that one's life purpose is the ultimate natural high. When it is being expressed to the world, you feel like you're
vibrating at a high level of consciousness where there is no need for substances
or activities that only provide us with a temporary and false high.

Every time we fulfill an addiction, we are choosing a place of trauma and pain within us instead of our purpose. We are saying, "I choose immediate comfort and gratification, even if it is taking me further away from my authentic self." Since addictions are a by-product of lacking purpose, they inevitably block us from experiencing any kind of lasting wellness and fulfillment. When we finally declare the importance of living with purpose beyond anything else, we are ready and willing to put our addictive behavior on the back burner.

Many of us are finally able to give up addictions when we put our purpose first. Interestingly, it can be an almost effortless process. As shown by quantum physics, every living thing vibrates at a certain energetic frequency. People that vibrate at a high frequency are self-actualized. They are fulfilling their sacred reason for being. People that vibrate at a low frequency are missing this core source of wisdom. Therefore, they are compelled to turn to external forces that match their low frequency. Addictions are one classification of low frequency forces. That is, they keep our life force subdued and our will to live suppressed. Your willingness to put your purpose first creates an immediate shift toward a higher energetic frequency. When this happens, your energetic nature is completely misaligned with that of addiction. There is no longer an energetic pull toward substances that keep us alienated from ourselves. In this way, the physical or mental craving almost spontaneously fades away. There is simply no one there to feed that compulsion any longer.

Almost all of us have succumbed to some sort of addictive or routinized behavior in our lives. Sure, many of us smoke, drink, or do drugs on a regular basis. Others choose shopping, gambling, TV watching, or food as their vice. But on a more subtle level, we are addicted to what we think and feel. We are addicted to our opinions, judgments, and attitudes. We are addicted to mechanically reenacting the same routine every day, to the same fights with our partner, to the same conversations with our friends, the same tendency toward gossip or judgment, the same actions that keep us feeling stuck where we are. When we look at the concept of addiction from this perspective, it becomes clear that *all of us suffer from addictive tendencies, whether on a subtle or overt level.*

LETTING GO OF ADDICTIONS IS
A GATEWAY TO ULTIMATE FREEDOM

We cannot honestly declare that our purpose is our first priority if we are not willing to let go of addictive behavior. Addictions are very effective at keeping our subconscious holding patterns intact. We simply can't access and liberate them if we are succumbing to addictive behavior. Once again, the key is to discover this place within yourself that is totally interested in evolving out of the stagnation that any form of addiction keeps you imprisoned in. Identify with this place of inner power and set the intention to be free of addiction without struggle. By doing this, you know that the payoff for peeling off a layer that has blocked your purpose is so much greater than the payoff you get from the temporary comfort that the addiction provides.

FIFTH OBSTACLE: Attachment to Distraction and Speed—The Outermost Layer that Forever Keeps Us at a Distance from Who We Are and Why We Are Here

The entire thrust of modern society is geared toward keeping us in a state of hyperdrive that prevents us from stopping and looking deeply at ourselves. In fact, it is almost taboo to spend prolonged periods of time in contemplation, simply observing the workings of the mind and considering the best way to live. Not only do we feel speed in our outer lives through our daily actions and responsibilities, we feel a hectic pace internally as well with our racing thoughts and anxious minds. When our minds are running a mile a minute, we will create a lifestyle that reflects this back to us, typically in the form of being excessively busy, constantly having to put out fires, or habitually distracting ourselves with the endless to-do list. Included in this obstacle is the vulnerability we have to filling our minds with useless information from sources such as television, the Internet, and mainstream magazines.

When we declare the importance of our purpose, we are consciously and deliberately slowing down in life to experience a simple level of being. Our purpose is invoked through receptivity and quietude, not through habitual stress and frenzied action. Many of us have learned that slowing down is a sign of laziness, that success comes from staying constantly busy. Chogyam Trungpa Rinpoche, a great spiritual teacher from Tibet, coined the term "the laziness of busyness" as a way to capture this belief and its effect on modern people. According to Trungpa, being excessively busy is actually considered a form of laziness if it prevents us from having a direct and open relationship with ourselves.

You may have had the experience of getting a high degree of external validation for being busy all of the time. You are praised by colleagues or friends as being a go-getter and you may have even been financially compensated for your efforts. The problem is that deep down, it feels like something is missing. This teaching on the "laziness of busyness" is a radical departure from participating in the frenetic activity that society rewards us for. It gives us permission to turn our awareness inward and spend consistent amounts of time in a state of reflection and "non-doing."

The distraction of speed is essentially another layer of addictive behavior that needs to be peeled away in order to tap into our purpose. We become addicted to the chaos, the noise, the frenetic movement of daily life. In fact, some of us actually feel that we thrive on this, that it enables us to feel important and productive. In this case, it's a good reminder that a lot of our most useful contributions and epiphanies come from pure silence. In fact, many of the greatest scientists, thinkers, and inventors have claimed that their ideas came through them in times of silence and meditation. The ability to remain in stillness is like an open door to our purpose, to who we really are. It helps us to merge with the reality that is much larger than our discursive, whirlwind thoughts that are bombarding us with a million different ideas about who we are and what we should do.

We can truly declare that we are ready for purpose when we can be with and enjoy ourselves without distraction.

Our lifestyle choices always reflect how attached we are to fear and negative beliefs. Whether it's our spouse, career, diet, or parenting style, our outer ways of being in the world tend to reinforce what we believe to be true in our inner world. There is always a relationship between our level of consciousness and the circumstances that are showing up in our lives. It is never random. Therefore, if you desire to change your outer circumstances, you also need to shift your consciousness. All of the following strategies will give you a step-by-step system for understanding how this works and, more importantly, how you can harmonize your inner and outer world to bring out your very best on all levels of being.

IGNORANCE IS NOT BLISS—OVERCOMING DENIAL IS MOVING CLOSER TO PURPOSE

It's important to point out here that we are only highlighting these obstacles to purpose so that we can let them go. The whole thrust of living with purpose is that we are entirely solution-oriented in our approach to life. We have no need to dwell on our problems, but we do need to clearly define what is preventing us from living fully. Once you have identified your major blocks to purpose, you can devote the rest of your life to liberating these blocks so you can experience freedom and offer it to others.

As you reflect upon these obstacles to purpose in your own life, know that you now have a very concrete reference point for what needs to change if you are to fulfill your true potential. If your tendency is to complicate life and make all of this talk about purpose overly abstract, or if you are telling yourself that you still don't get what it means to put your purpose first, you can start with peeling away the outer two layers of the onion: lifestyle choices that perpetuate speed and distraction, and addictions. Keep it simple. That is always the key to tapping into your purpose.

CASE STUDY ⚜ HELEN ⚜

Helen came to my acupuncture practice with a host of medical and personal problems. She had recently made a full recovery from breast cancer but was suffering from chronic fatigue and bouts of depression. She also reported a host of digestive problems, poor sleep, impaired circulation, and a sluggish metabolism.

In her personal life, Helen had been struggling to adapt to a new job that felt overwhelming to her. She was also witnessing the gradual demise of her ex-husband due to a chronic illness. Lastly, she felt that her relationship with her two adult children was strained and that she was never able to connect with them as well as she would have liked.

Even though Helen came to my practice with a litany of issues, I could tell right away that the prognosis for healing was great. What is most important in forming a prognosis for any patient is not the extent of their problems, but their relationship with what is causing them pain. In Helen's case, she was finally at a place with herself where she was ready to accept full responsibility for the life she had created. She was not hiding behind any excuses, nor was she blaming anyone or anything for her hardship.

In so many words, she came to me and said, "I'm ready. I want to claim a new life for myself, even if it's scary or feels hard." Helen's lifestyle was largely promoting her feelings of imbalance. She was addicted to sugar and drank a couple cups of strong coffee every morning. She didn't exercise much, nor did she make time to consciously relax in her life.

continued

Even though she was steeped in some life-denying habits, she was ready to change. Helen made a number of fairly dramatic dietary changes and started doing yoga and meditation several times a week. She also hired a personal trainer and committed to brisk walking on a regular basis. Through life coaching and acupuncture, she took the necessary steps to heal her relationship with her kids.

In every area of her life, Helen decided to take full responsibility for herself. She had had enough of compulsively reacting to what life was bringing her. She was ready to live with purpose in all areas of her life, even though that meant letting go of some very old and familiar habits and beliefs. Because of this, she literally reinvented herself. She lost 20 pounds and began to look several years younger. The chronic depression began to give way to a very youthful joy that was contagious to those around her. She settled into her job and actually began to enjoy it. Every facet of her life began to flow in a new and wonderful way. This could only have happened by her being willing to look at herself with ruthless honesty.

OK, any questions about the fourth strategy?

This all sounds great, but what if the main obstacle that I discover is that I simply don't believe that my life has a purpose?

First and foremost, you have to honestly assess for yourself how that belief is working for you. By not believing that your life has a purpose, do you feel inspired, connected, awake, joyful, and appreciative? Probably not. In order to put the Purpose Principle to work in your life, you have to be willing to suspend even this belief and hang out in some unknown territory. Your willingness to do this will only come from clearly seeing how painful it is to hold on to this belief and the subsequent futility you feel in trying to create some sort of happiness in your life.

Attaching to a belief that life has no purpose is like starving ourselves to death when we are surrounded by a bounty of food. Everything we need to nourish and sustain ourselves is right in front of us, but we have to choose to acknowledge it. Ultimately, this belief is one of the small self's many ways to try and assert some basic control over life and act as if it knows what this whole affair called existence is about. Unfortunately, whatever control we feel is at the sacrifice of our sacred purpose and the bountiful qualities that arise out of it, such as creativity, beauty, and fulfillment.

Mere belief implies separation. If you believe in it, you are separate from whatever you believe in. In this sense, we see that even attaching to positive beliefs can get us in trouble. After all, what if something happens that directly conflicts with what we believe to be true? The fullest expression of life purpose, however, is a complete unification with our deepest essence and reason for being. It transcends belief. Life purpose comes when we let go of our conditioned beliefs entirely, whether they appear to be positive or negative.

One last thing. Can you hold within yourself the possibility that you can access a newfound freedom when you drop the attachment to the belief that your life is meaningless? Can you see how this belief is pigeonholing the enormity of this universe into such a narrow and limiting perspective? It is important to bring this up, because you are certainly not alone if you have felt this way. Many people share this feeling. It is by default a by-product of our excessive focus on the physical world as the only reality.

If you are ready to move on to the next strategy and suspend your beliefs for this period of time, you are to be admired. That alone is a big step.

I have been told that I drink too much. I feel like alcohol opens me up and makes me more creative. I am not one of those people who passes out watching TV. Instead, I feel like drinking helps me connect more with myself. I have new ideas and insights and feel more lighthearted. It seems to bring me closer to my purpose. Why do I need to give it up?

By their nature, addictions fill us up with qualities that we feel are lacking without them. In this case, you do not feel connected and creative without alcohol. Life purpose, on the other hand, is the innate experience of these qualities as the natural expression of who you really are. Any reliance on an external source will only weaken your access to this innate treasure that lies within you. In the situation you are describing, part of your life purpose is to experience the qualities of connection, creativity, and lightheartedness as being part of your innate essence without any need for alcohol as a way to access it. In this way, you willingly invite every belief and perception into your conscious life that prevents you from this experience. As you move closer to this ultimate source of connection and lightness within you, you begin to see that whatever seeming benefit you have received from drinking pales in comparison to the expression of your life purpose.

I gave up smoking a few years ago and was proud of myself for that accomplishment. I soon realized, however, that I was eating a lot more and that I was addicted to food. I ended up gaining a lot of weight and then decided that I needed to get in shape. I stopped eating so much and started exercising regularly. After a while, I became obsessed with exercise and felt like I had to work out every day. I seem to be able to give up one addiction, only to have it be replaced with another form of addiction almost immediately. Why is this?

Until the underlying reason why you were compelled to seek out addictions in the first place is addressed, the cycle of addiction will continue and can easily migrate to new forms. It doesn't matter whether it's shopping, food, exercise, smoking, cocaine, sex, or the Internet, the underlying cycle of addictive behavior has to be examined. We turn to addictions when we are attached to belief systems that promote fear, insecurity, and separation. We seek out external solutions to shield us from the trauma we have felt in our lives. The addiction gives us a way to cope with and feel in control of the world we live in. Until we meet these underlying beliefs head on, this cycle can only continue.

I know some people who seem to be addicted to living a very healthy and pure life. They will only eat organic foods. They would never consider indulging in a doughnut or a greasy piece of pizza. Is it possible to have an addiction to being healthy?

Living with purpose means that we are willing to finally and fully renounce all addictive behavior. In this case, we can easily become identified with eating a certain way and living a certain lifestyle. The problem is that, if these conditions were taken away, we would very likely feel quite anxious and distraught. Life purpose is, first and foremost, an unconditional experience of who we really are. Its foundation is not dependent on eating or living a certain way. While it is true that purposeful people want to take care of their health, they are not attached to food or other lifestyle factors. They know that the ultimate source of nourishment is being in direct contact with life purpose, even more so than the quality of food they eat or the air they breathe.

EXERCISES

1 Take an honest look at the way your parents raised you. What were the main beliefs that were instilled in you from early childhood? What examples did they set in the home through their actions? What emotions were most prevalent? How did you feel as a child in your home environment? Even if they were subtle, can you detect any harmful beliefs that were embedded within you?

2 To what extent have you completely liberated any damaging beliefs that were instilled in you? Without judging yourself, just notice how fully independent you are of the way you were raised. Have you been able to free yourself from your childhood blueprint?

3 Look at the ways you waste time or postpone what's truly meaningful to you. Can you call out that voice in your head that convinces you that you can work on the core issues of your life at some point later on? Where do you negotiate with yourself to settle for a circumstance that is misaligned with fulfillment, prosperity, or love? What excuses do you make as to why you need to continue on with this?

4 Take a look at any addictions that you have not overcome. What is preventing you from freeing yourself from them in this moment? (Whatever excuse may arise, apply the fifth strategy to it).

5 Think and declare for yourself, say it out loud, and ask for assistance: "I am ready for my purpose. It is more important than anything else. I am more committed to this than anything else." Keep this declaration with you at all times. Hold it in your heart.

FREE Your Obstacles by Focusing on Space

Problems can't be solved by the same level of thinking that created them.

—Albert Einstein

We cannot change anything unless we accept it. Condemnation does not liberate, it oppresses.

—Carl Jung

The previous strategy was about the willingness we must have to look at each and every obstacle that stands in the way of our purpose. In this strategy, we are moving in the direction of freeing ourselves from these obstacles and any substandard aspects of our current reality that don't match up with our purpose.

These quotes by Einstein and Jung profoundly summarize the perspective we must embrace in order to actively embark on a life of purpose and fulfillment. Most of us have an exceptionally difficult time with changing ourselves for the better. We try to go on a diet, only to have success for a period of time, then have the whole project blow up in our face as we experience a massive rebellion against the "right way to eat." We try to attain more wealth only to land back in the same financial plateau over and over. Or we do end up acquiring more wealth only to realize it was at the grave sacrifice of our marriage and home life. We finally think we have found our dream job only to realize that it is a different form of the same mediocrity that we have subjected ourselves to time and again. We try to improve our self-esteem with positive affirmations only to discover that our internal B.S. detector is fully charged, ready to pounce on any contrived self-affirmations with an increasingly powerful arsenal of negative and defeatist thoughts.

A CRUCIAL PIECE OF THE PURPOSE PUZZLE

Declaring the importance of our purpose truly is just the first step. Now, we have to know how to relate with all of the obstacles that we see as a result of asking for purpose. Put simply, we have to know how to relate to our reality as it currently stands, given that it is likely out of alignment with the reality we really want, the one that is closer to who we really are.

This is where a lot of people get stopped dead in their tracks on the path to self-discovery. We know that something needs to be changed, that our life isn't measuring up to what we would like it to be. We may even declare out loud that we're ready to unite with our purpose, ready to surrender what is holding us back. But here is where we get hung up:

We try to find our purpose in the same way that we have tried to do everything else in our life, which just so happens to be the exact mechanism that has caused us to stray from our purpose in the first place.

Read that sentence a few times. What this means is that, in order to live with purpose, we have to come from a new place within. We can't just rely on the same habitual motivations and thought patterns that caused us to suffer in the first place. We have to be willing to surrender to a new inner resource, one that is not at all identified with how we have done things to this point. What is this resource?

SPACE: THE HIDDEN SOLUTION THAT'S ALWAYS AVAILABLE

Space is a beautiful concept. It is the missing piece of the psychological puzzle for so many modern people. We can be incredibly smart, talented, ambitious, motivated, and clever, but still be miserable or dissatisfied. Why? Because we don't have space. Without space, there is no breathing room in our awareness. We suffocate ourselves in a narrowly confined passageway that shrinks who we are down to a tiny pebble. This pebble is surrounded by infinite space, but we habitually identify only with the pebble as who we are. We try to change ourselves within the confines of this pebble, which means we can only evolve to the outer edges of this very small psychological environment that we have created. Amazingly, there is an infinite ocean of spacious, light, and flowing energy to tap into beyond this tiny pebble, but we have to be aware of and take an interest in this infinite ocean or else it will forever remain outside of our framework of living.

What we are essentially developing space around is thought and emotion. We are breaking free of the incessant noise made by our judging mind, which is fueled by the small self. When we tap into space, we no longer buy into our thoughts and feelings. We no longer believe that our true Self is bound up in our head. Ultimately, we are creating space around any tendency we have to attach to things as being solid, real, or a certain way. Remember, attachment is the ultimate obstacle. And we can't find the solution to that obstacle with more attachment.

This fifth strategy is about seeing beyond the pebble reality into this vast field of potential that underlies and surrounds each moment. How do we do this? (Remember, the answer to this question can only arise when we are ready. It is 100% based on our willingness to put purpose first). The best approach here is steeped in simplicity. All that you are going to do is be present with whatever arises from here on out with nothing but acceptance and awareness. You are simply going to be aware of what is taking place inside of you without any sort of fixed agenda on changing it, making it go away, blindly reacting to it, or doing anything at all with it.

OBSERVING WITHOUT REACTING

To observe without evaluating is the highest form of intelligence.

— K r i s h n a m u r t i

This is a radical step for most of us. When we are face to face with an aspect of ourselves that feels uncomfortable or painful, our habitual reaction is to find a way to make it go away. We resist it or we crave something other than it. And that is how we try to change it. We try to will into reality its destruction or we force into being a new stimulus (such as an addiction or a distraction) that serves to bury it. On the other end of the spectrum, when we finally feel more positive, we try to hold on to that feeling as long as we can. We crave it. This is the exact mechanism within each of us that causes us to suffer. We resist what we don't like and we crave what we do like.

This fifth strategy is about simply bearing witness to who you are and the reality you have as it currently stands. No fixation on changing it, no attachment to denying it, no impulse to resist it. You are, for the first time ever, simply letting it be. We are giving a tremendous amount of space to the obstacles around our purpose: our self-hatred, laziness, negativity, addictions, traumas, and even the positive states of mind such as happiness, pleasure, or peace. We are not trying to change any of it. Instead, we are letting the entire spectrum of our experience arise and pass away without trying to wish it were different than it is or cling to it as something permanent. No need to do anything whatsoever with it. Space. Ahhhh.

When we resist the life that we currently have, we only feed our perceived problems. You have probably heard the statement, "what you resist persists." This is absolutely true. What you focus on will indeed expand in your life. If you are focused on all of the problems you have in your current reality regardless of what they are, you will only get more of the same in the future. This is the unfortunate and very painful cycle that many of us get stuck in for what can be countless years. It is like the hamster that keeps spinning on the wheel, thinking that if it just goes a little faster, it will get somewhere other than where it is. But all that happens is we feel more desperate, exhausted, and discouraged each time we fruitlessly return to the same point of origin.

Space is the beginning of the end of this torturous process. Space is the ultimate antidote to any momentum in life that veers away from our purpose. Space is what enables you to finally drop the conflict you have with yourself. It enables you to start anew, to refresh yourself, and utilize a much more sane and empowering resource that resides within you. Let's look at a few examples to see how this works:

You are stuck in traffic on your way to work. You are already a few minutes late and you can feel the stress mounting in your body. Your heart is beating fast and your muscles are tightening up. There is a surge of anger arising within you, as you realize you are at the mercy of the thousands of cars around you. You want to scream, to pound your fist through the windshield and say, "Would all you f***ng idiots get out of my way?"

Let's give this situation space. You feel all of the anger, the lack of control, the stress, and you don't react to it, you don't identify with it, and you don't try to change it. Instead you say, "It is what it is. So be it." You acknowledge your feelings. Then you consciously relax your body. You take a few deep breaths. You even bring a smile to your face, knowing that in the infinite scheme of things, this one incident is relatively trivial. You use this as an opportunity to stay awake to what is happening without any agenda to change it. Tapping into the infinite space of the situation is predicated upon recognizing that you have a choice in how you will relate to it.

Perhaps the next extension of this process would be the spontaneous recognition that you are repeatedly late to your job for a legitimate reason: You simply don't like it. As you open to the space around you, there is a palpable recognition that you are forcing yourself to go to a job every day that you really have no interest in. No wonder you're late! You can bring some compassion to your tardiness. As you further open up to the moment and its infinite spaciousness, you may even be overtaken by a brief flash of the life you *really* want. You may feel it in your bones, if even just for a second. All of this from a willingness to drop the resistance. That is how purpose is awakened within us.

IN EVERY SITUATION, NO MATTER HOW DIFFICULT, WE CAN CHOOSE TO FOCUS ON THE SPACE THAT SURROUNDS IT

Let's say you've been stuck at home with your two-year-old son all day long. With his incessant whining and relentless crying, he has kept you in a state of mild annoyance and irritation for most of the day. Just looking at him makes your nervous system feel like it's being shredded by a cheese grater. You call your spouse at the office and make a few snippy comments at them, not so subtly suggesting that your disdain for this situation is all their fault.

As you hang up the phone, you suddenly notice that the house is quiet. Thinking that something bad must have happened, you rush into your son's room and see that he is totally absorbed in one of his toy trucks. The look of exquisite curiosity on his face makes all of the pain of the day miraculously melt away. You suddenly remember what a gift he is in your life and how fortunate you are to have him. It hits you like a ton of bricks that you haven't been present with him at all on this day.

In the very next moment, he starts to cry again. Instead of reacting with more annoyance, you go over and sit with him and give him your fullest attention. Amazingly, the crying stops and you see that this is what he wanted from you all along.

THE NATURAL CULTIVATION OF GRATITUDE

Something quite interesting begins to happen when you cultivate some space around your current reality. You breathe more deeply, you feel more patient, you have more trust, and most importantly, you begin to feel a natural welling up of gratitude for who you are and where you are at in your life. Most of us have heard how important it is to express appreciation for life, that it is a crucial ingredient in order to attract the life that we really want. But how do we feel gratitude when there is so much resistance to our current situation? We can't force appreciation for ourselves when our thoughts and feelings pretty much suggest the opposite most of the time. We can't say, "I appreciate this extra 20 pounds," when in reality we desperately want it to go away and we feel hatred toward it. We can't say, "I appreciate this job," when in fact we loathe going to work every day.

So how does gratitude factor into our current situation? It is indeed an essential part of the equation for a life of fulfillment and optimum wellness. In fact, it is one of the most important attributes we can develop within ourselves on the path to life purpose. But it certainly cannot be forced into existence. That is just more of the same dynamic that has created our suffering. Instead of forcing or contriving a state of gratitude, try this:

Cultivate gratitude for the simple recognition of the space around your current reality.

Because there is nothing fixed or solid about your current reality, you can feel grateful. By bringing this quality of space to—and cutting through the momentum of—your obstacles to purpose, you see that these obstacles were never real in the first place. You see that you have a natural ability to transform these obstacles in a moment simply by bringing nonjudgmental attention to what is happening. Because there is infinite potential to drop suffering right now and to genuinely transform what isn't working in your life, you can feel grateful. Because everything is constantly changing, you can feel grateful. The recognition of space fills you with gratitude. Even deeper, the recognition that you have a choice to cultivate space fills you with gratitude. You now know that you can relate to any situation, no matter how difficult, with compassion. You can feel grateful for the enormous reality that lies beyond the confined pebble version of yourself that you have been stuck in. By cultivating gratitude, you are embracing the most direct, genuine, and potent means you have as a human being to develop the qualities of freedom and generosity within your own being.

When you begin to see that everything is workable because nothing is solid or permanent, you feel gratitude. You bring appreciation to the illusory nature of your struggles. You can look at your debt and appreciate the space around that situation, the potential for it to change. You can look at a failed marriage and recognize the potential for that pain to wake you up and help you evolve, to shed light on the lesson that you've needed to learn. You feel grateful for that. Expressing gratitude is based on the understanding that every single life event can bring us closer to our purpose. Gratitude results from the realization that we have a choice to relate to each moment with awareness, care, and openness.

This is a radically new approach for most of us in the modern world. Instead of fighting against what is, we cultivate space around it, then have gratitude for our ability to do this. Simple yet amazing. Whatever current struggle you are experiencing, use this step right now to initiate change in the most empowering and authentic way possible.

CUTTING THROUGH THE MOMENTUM

Much of what keeps our pain intact and makes it seem so solid is the momentum that has been built up through years of recurring thoughts, feelings, and actions. When you focus on space, you are essentially cutting through the momentum of habits that can be deeply ingrained. In any moment, *the absolute first thing to do is to stop doing anything at all and just observe what is happening.* Pay attention without attachment. Notice what the momentum is without judging it. Feel in your body what is happening.

WHEN YOU:
- Feel the impulse to shout at your spouse, cut the momentum.
- Are reaching for that third helping of Ben & Jerry's, cut the momentum.
- Are curled up in bed and feel unmotivated to face the day, cut the momentum.
- Are about to say something judgmental or harsh about someone, cut the momentum.

In every moment, you can choose to expand your consciousness by cutting any habitual momentum that is gearing you up for further contraction. You can use the incredibly powerful faculty of your own awareness to return to a place of expansion again and again. In each moment that we live, our primary purpose is always to return to this state of expansion by cutting through the momentum of habit and contraction.

In any moment, you can do this. It is such a simple step that we can easily overlook it. Remember, your ability to do this is 100% predicated upon the level of your awareness and how willing you are to let go into the space that surrounds your thoughts and emotions.

THE PROCESS OF CHANGE

As mentioned earlier, becoming aware of the space around our current reality is a radically new step for so many of us, especially since we are so deeply conditioned to solve our problems with the same approaches that caused the problems in the first place. Since this is new territory, let's anticipate some of the experiences we may have as we surrender to what is.

When you put your purpose first, you are allowing in a tiny flicker of intense light that is full of your brilliance, genius, and limitless potential. At first, this tiny flicker will appear to be vulnerable to the habitual self within you that has created a foundation of life that, by and large, you now intend to transform. It can feel like there is 1% of you that wants this change (the flicker of light) and 99% of you that honestly has no interest in it whatsoever or fights like hell against it (the small self). As you try to quit smoking or drinking or transition out of a job or marriage that isn't working, whatever it is, there is this small flicker of potential within you that knows this is the right way to go. It has no doubt. It only wants to evolve. This other large edifice of conditioned behavior, however, is chock-full of doubt, ambivalence, and fear.

Bringing space to your current reality means that you are going to keep your focus on this 1% flicker that is your purpose-based Self. It's not that it needs to battle with the other 99% of you that wants to stay the same. The purpose-based Self has no interest in conflict or struggle. This is a crucial point:

Anytime you notice that you are caught in a struggle of trying to change yourself, improve yourself, or identify with this 1% flicker, your focus is on the small self. Struggle = small self.

Don't forget, this little opening of purpose you have glimpsed has no interest in internal conflict. You don't have to work really hard or fight with yourself to experience this flicker. It is your natural state. You simply have to bring space to the 99% of you that feels conflicted, depressed, anxious, whatever it is. Stop trying to improve it or make it feel better. Stop trying to understand it. Then, keep your focus on that 1%. No conflict. No fighting with yourself. No resistance.

As you do this, that 1% flicker becomes 2%. The more you bring space to your struggle and keep your focus on your purpose, you feed your real nature and it flourishes more and more. Eventually, it shines through you and everything you do and completely overrides this small, wounded self that is full of conflict. As this process unfolds, your external world will always accurately mirror back to you your level of internal realization. Old friends that are no longer a good match for you drop out of your life. A job that no longer resonates with your true nature spontaneously drops away and a new situation presents itself. We call this process synchronicity.

To summarize, your job is to focus on the infinite space that surrounds anything that is showing up in your life that you don't want, whether it's anger, fear, pain, depression, laziness, addictions, toxic relationships, or a mediocre job. By keeping your focus on the space around these forces, you will stop the painful cycle of strengthening them through resistance. It does not stop here. You also need to bring space to anything that is showing up in your life that you do want, that you crave more of. Craving and resistance are two sides of the same coin. Bring space to even the positive thoughts, feelings, and circumstances you have. By focusing on space in this way, you are cutting through the momentum of whatever it is that you don't want and you are freeing (not holding on to) that which you do want, which is exactly what you need to do to prevent the cycle of struggle, mediocrity, or distress from continually recurring.

A NEW KIND OF DISCIPLINE

In a certain way, many of us will find this to be the most challenging step that we ever embark on because it is so foreign to our built-in sensibilities and beliefs. This strategy requires a kind of discipline that is based on the process of surrender, not trying harder. It is the discipline of peeling off the layers of who we are, of letting go into deeper levels of our being. This kind of discipline requires courage and an earnest desire to unleash the fullest expression of our human potential.

Even though it is, as mentioned, the most challenging thing we can do in this life, we can never get stuck in the belief that it is hard. In reality, it is only hard to the small self. Not only is it hard, it is impossible. To the purpose-based Self, however, the discipline of surrender is not hard at all; it is completely natural. Any time you find yourself saying how hard it is to make changes from this place of fullness, remember that it is only your small self talking in those moments. If you identify with this process as being difficult, the odds are that you will once again return to the familiar place of pain and separation. When we focus on space, we cannot be attached to any sort of small self-based label.

CASE STUDY ❀ SANDRA ❀

Sandra came to my acupuncture practice on the verge of a nervous breakdown. Her personal and professional life was in a state of turmoil. Sandra's daughter was suicidal and had already tried to take her life on two occasions. Active in the political scene, Sandra was caught in a web of dysfunction with a colleague who was continually trying to undermine her authority. Sandra was also involved in a distressing situation with a friend who co-owned a property with her. This friend had on several occasions exhibited bizarre and disturbing behavior that made Sandra call into question her own safety.

Sandra's overwhelming impulse in her life was to fight for what she felt was right and just. Whatever life brought her, she would meet with a ferocious need to make the situation right. She poured an enormous amount of effort into getting her daughter to take the right course of action in her life. She fought with an intense will to bring justice to the political environment she was working in.

Interestingly, Sandra approached her impending nervous breakdown with the same intensity and fight that she did everything else in her life. She looked at it as a competition against herself to find a way to correct her feelings of collapse. When I had Sandra examine why she attracted so much turmoil and chaos into her life, she began to make a remarkable discovery. She realized that she had a habitual need to make things right and that by bringing in so much hardship, she was always put in a position of being the problem solver, which she had formed her identity around.

Unfortunately, this habit had led to a life of continual distress and drama. Even worse, the only way she knew how to address her distress was through the exact same approach that had caused it in the first place.

Over the course of several acupuncture and life coaching sessions, Sandra began to soften her edges and consider the possibility that she could find a genuine strength in releasing her need to find justice in every situation. Her practice was to bring space to this lifelong habit that had attracted such tumult and pain and to embrace a quality of her being that was vulnerable and compassionate.

By bringing her focus to the space around this ancient pattern, Sandra was able to make miraculous changes within a few weeks. She developed healthy boundaries with her daughter and stopped trying to control her actions and emotions; she quit her job in a very dignified way that gave her a great deal of peace and satisfaction; and she bought out her neurotic friend's share of their property and severed ties with her.

Amazingly, by creating space around this harmful pattern, Sandra was able to effortlessly attract a healthy relationship into her life for the first time ever. She experienced a 180-degree turnaround in her life, all by bringing space to the pattern that was causing herself and others so much harm.

It is really crucial that we understand this lesson, as it is indeed an entryway to the life we really want. Let's field some questions before we move on.

Sometimes I feel like I have to fight against any undesirable circumstances I have because that is the way I know how to change them. It sounds like creating space would be a form of giving up and saying that the things I don't want are allowed to win. What am I missing here?

There is a world of difference between spiritual acceptance and blind resignation. Bringing space to our lives is a way of deeply accepting present moment reality as it is, because to do otherwise would only create harm. Since this moment is the reality we have, it is far better to surround it with a spacious kind of acceptance and nonviolence than it is to react to it with force, rejection, or hatred. Sure, we know that we want something better out of life. But since this moment is all we have, even if it's not what we want, we treat it with surrender. As we do this, we can put our focus on to what we really want, which is covered in the next strategy. Quite contrary to giving up and allowing negativity to win, this is the wisest and most effective way to free ourselves from anything that is showing up in our lives that does not serve us. Instead of trying to change ourselves from a ground of self-rejection, we are starting with the ground of humble acceptance and love. In this way, our cup is already full as we bring to fruition what we really want.

So, if I've tried to give up smoking ten times before but always end up going back to it, I am obviously trying to clear out the addiction with the same motivation that created it in the first place, right?

Yes.

If I want to try and quit again, what does it mean to give space to the addiction? I want to make sure I get this.

Most likely, when you tried to quit each time before, you would use a high degree of will power to force yourself to stop quitting. Since will power will always run out, you are brought back to into the addictive behavior because you didn't know what else you could draw from internally that would help you through the pain of quitting. Creating space means that you are willing to contact a new resource inside of yourself that is not based on will power or force. Instead, you could say it is a place of genuine power within you that *knows* that smoking is not in alignment with who you really are.

When you put your focus on this knowing, you would start right now to relate to smoking in an entirely new way. You would really feel and be present to that habitual, small, cramped part of yourself that wants another cigarette. You would notice the satisfaction that this small self gets when smoking. But, by putting your focus on the space around that small self, you are no longer identified with it as who you are. You see through it. This all starts with putting your purpose first and being willing to see outside of this small self that clings to the comfort of smoking.

Now, this does not mean that quitting smoking will be completely smooth sailing. You will still experience the same physical and emotional withdrawals. But now you have identified with this place inside of you that is no longer aligned with smoking, this place that is so much larger than the life-depleting nature of cigarettes. By keeping your focus here, you have an inner resource of strength to draw from when the cravings are at their strongest. So there is a quality of effortlessness to it because smoking is no longer a natural reflection of who you are.

Although we used smoking as the example here, you can pretty much fill in the blank with anything in your life that is not working right now, whether it's financial issues, a boring job, a dissatisfying marriage, or other kinds of addictions. The key here is that you become extremely interested in this place of purpose within yourself that is in no way bound to the painful circumstances you seek escape from. This place of purpose is what will enable you to bring an entirely different energy forth so you can actually free yourself of problems rather than perpetuating them with your small self.

In this way, we are finally seeing that anything outside of ourselves isn't really the problem. In this case, smoking isn't the real issue. The only problem is that our inner reality is out of alignment with our purpose, with the infinite space of the universe that is who we really are to begin with. Smoking merely symbolizes that we are out of touch with this inner power. So we need to start by shifting our inner reality instead of trying to force ourselves to quit smoking. If we quit smoking without making this inner shift, the addiction will only migrate to another form and will likely make us even more irritable or anxious.

EXERCISES

1   Make a list of all of the things that frustrate you about yourself: your body, your finances, your marriage, or anything else that you want to change about your life.

2   Pay very close attention to the way your body feels and to the nature of your thoughts as you focus on these life themes that you want to change. In particular, notice any feelings of contraction in your muscles and difficult emotions (anger, longing, sadness, grief) that well up within you as you focus on what you want to change.

3   See if you can let all of these feelings and sensations just float in space. You are just observing them without any conflict or resistance. Just let them be. You can use your breathing to facilitate this process. Breathing in deeply, feel the space of your breath open up your body. Breathing out deeply, gently feel the tension in yourself releasing.

4   As you do this, declare to yourself throughout this process that you are ready to activate your true purpose. Ask for this all day long, but do so without any resistance to what you currently have and who you currently are.

5   When was the last time you looked up at the sky and contemplated the vastness of outer space? This is a simple and immediate way to expand your awareness and get a sense of the reality that is beyond the tiny pebble of "I" that we have talked about in this strategy.

6   Put a glass or similar object on a table in front of you. See if you can focus your attention on the space that is between you and the glass. Now, see if you can create the same kind of focus on the space between you and your thoughts.

Now that you are becoming familiar with the space that always surrounds your thoughts and feelings, let's talk about how to use the power of your mind in an astonishingly new and very helpful way.

FREE Your Mind Through Awakened Imagination

Imagination will often carry us to worlds that never were. But without it we go nowhere.

—Carl Sagan

When a fantasy turns you on, you're obligated to God and nature to start doing it—right away.

—Stewart Brand

Now, the fun part begins.

What we have done through the previous strategies is create a fertile ground to start working with the amazing power of our imagination. We have cleared our inner landscape so that we are no longer enslaved by self-imposed limitations. We are once again open to infinite possibility, to the unlimited potential that lies dormant at the core of our Being, just waiting to be aroused.

Going back to the way that you were raised, do you remember that your parents and schooling gave you the tools to develop your imagination? Was this at all encouraged? Unfortunately, most of us were basically shown that imagination is a rather useless faculty that will only get us in trouble. We are taught to put all our eggs in the basket of intellect and are assured that this is the way to life's bounty. Imagination, we are taught, is an irresponsible construct of the mind that has no bearing on a successful and prosperous life.

How tragic this is! As you will see, imagination is our primary asset for becoming solution-oriented and empowered. It directly links us to a place of inner freedom, resourcefulness, and joy. It is the most powerful faculty we have to create the life that we really want, for we have to first imagine the manifestation of our purpose before we can live it.

The recognition of infinite space we discussed in the fifth strategy is a beckoning to activate our imagination so we can start envisioning who we really are and what we really want out of life. When we focus on space, we give ourselves the opportunity to enjoy a blank slate, a no-holds-barred, free-for-all brainstorming on the creation of our ideal life. Up to this point in life, we have likely used our imagination in a way that actually works against us. We have imagined ourselves to be a limited and conflicted being who doesn't feel safe or connected to life. Or we have imagined ourselves to be someone who just deserves what they have, as if it's blasphemous to ask for more out of life.

When we are being run by the subconscious holding patterns described in the fourth strategy, we cannot use our imagination to our benefit. It will only work against us because our imagination can only conceive of the limiting emotions and beliefs that are still swirling around in our subconscious. To harness the amazing benefit of our imagination, our focus must be on the limitless space that surrounds all of the pain or obstacles we have felt up to this point.

It's important to recognize that we really do imagine our self-image and the reality that we have, even though it seems so real. The main suggestion here is that you can start right now to awaken more beauty and abundance into your life simply by changing the focus of what you imagine yourself to be.

How do we do this? By asking the right questions.

Stop wasting your time, ask the big questions.

— G e n p o   R o s h i

The questions we ask of ourselves determine the avenue that our imagination goes down. The following questions take us down a dead-end path, as they inevitably lead back to the same frustrating place of pain over and over:

❧ Why am I so fat?

❧ I know I should just bear down and find a way to like my job, but I just can't seem to do it. What the heck is wrong with me?

❧ I hate this debt. What in the world can I do to make it go away?

❧ I just can't stand getting hurt by men anymore. Why don't they want to be with me? Is it because I'm just not that attractive?

❧ How do I make this pain in my body go away?

We can take this down to a much more mundane level as well:

❧ Where in the hell did I put my car keys? I always lose those damn things.

These are the kinds of questions most of us have been trained to ask ourselves in order to initiate change in life, whether it's finding our car keys or finding true love. They come from a place of subconscious trauma and they can only bring us back to that same point of origin again and again. You can see that the underlying energy within each of these questions is steeped in resistance and aversion. We don't want what we have or who we are, so we try to conjure up a way to improve our situation. We end up using our imagination as a way to keep us bound up in the small self. The way that we are using our minds keeps us blocked from the infinite space that surrounds this pebble reality. When we ask questions in this way, we are like the hamster spinning endlessly around the wheel. We keep returning to the same circumstances over and over: same extra weight, same lousy job, same crippling debt, same betrayal in relationships, same old chronic pain in our bodies and, yes, same missing car keys.

ON AN ULTIMATE LEVEL,
OUR PROBLEMS DON'T EXIST

When we remain stuck in our focus on our problems, it feels like it will take a monumental effort to make them go away. In reality, we feel this way because we can't make our problems go away if our only reference point for change is the problems themselves. But when we ask the right questions, our imagination is given permission to completely drop our identification with our problems. Without any effort at all, but a basic willingness to do so, we shift our focus from what is wrong with us to what we really want. We become solution-oriented instead of problem-oriented.

When we invoke the liberating power of our imagination, we mercifully realize that *our problems don't really exist.* They are created out of our small, pebble self that is attached to narrow viewpoints about reality. Your problems are completely dependent upon your perceptions. If you change your perceptions by asking new questions of yourself, you will immediately see that there is nothing ultimately wrong. A problem-oriented perspective cannot see beyond the physical world. It uses all of the worldly suffering—war, famine, injustice, and stress—as evidence to support its assertion that there is no true refuge. Just keep trying harder or, at some point, just give up entirely. It is hopeless. This world is full of problems and that's just the way it is. We feel powerless to change it because it is all that we perceive. The only place our imagination goes is to "the problem."

A solution-oriented perspective is one that is deeply connected to the invisible world of the imagination, which is an open door to this undamaged, completely awake and liberated place that every single person has within them. It does not ignore what happens in physical reality. Being solution-oriented does not mean that we are blind to what is happening. Instead, it means bringing a different focus to light that enables us to see that in every so-called problem, there is a completely spacious and open reality that surrounds it. We can feel the pain of the problem, then put our focus on this expansive perception of the space that it is floating in.

Our imagination is finally allowed to soar when we recognize the space around our current reality, the limitless potential that is at the essence of each moment. When we taste this space, we tap into a new faculty within ourselves that can immediately take us to new heights. It is like a door is blown open within us that takes us to a room without walls, and we finally realize the wide-open nature of our own being. That is how the imagination flourishes. It isn't really "you" anymore who is imagining. Instead, your being is like a vessel that connects to the greater universe. Life moves through this vessel, but it is not you. Indeed, your imagination is linked to the reality that goes way beyond "you." It is not personal anymore. Moving through this door is our first real taste of freedom.

AWAKENING DORMANT FACULTIES

Out of this shift in our perception through imagination, all kinds of dormant faculties begin to awaken within us. Imagination is the doorway to:

- Enhanced creativity
- The expression of genius
- A greater love and appreciation for all that we are and can be

- An ability to inspire others
- Youthfulness and boundless energy
- The greatest discoveries of humankind
- Anything that we truly desire
- Our ideal life

When we ask the right questions, we are finally able to assess with crystal clarity what it is that we really want. The only way that we can create a blessed and abundant life is to know what we're really looking for and then put our focus there. To know what we're really looking for, we have to clear out all of the obstacles and extract our real Self from all of the wayward voices within us that want so many conflicting things. We have to be unified in ourselves to know what we want. This is where a lot of us get hung up. We set goals and intentions and even visualize what we want coming to fruition. Then we are frustrated and disappointed, possibly even left feeling betrayed, when reality does not conform to what we are envisioning in our minds. We think, "Oh, all this goal-setting and visualization stuff is nonsense. I'll just go back to working my ass off and doing the best I can."

When the universe does not seem to grant us what we are asking for, the problem is that we are not unified within ourselves. We don't know ourselves intimately enough to clearly assess what we really want. Instead, we put out a lot of mixed messages. Let's say you own a business and have set goals and intentions around bringing in a flock of new customers. Deep down though, you feel pretty burned out with how much you're already taking on. Part of you is asking for more, part of you is asking for less. Part of this is conscious, part is subconscious.

This is how many of us live every day of our lives. We are fragmented in the way we choose to live and in what we ask of the universe. This is because we are entangled in a lot of harmful beliefs about ourselves that keep the cage of conflict intact.

Activating the amazing faculty of imagination happens when we unlock this cage by seeing the space around it. We can now discern what we're looking for from a place of unlimited potential. We learn how to ask for and visualize the things that will bring us closer to our purpose, the things that make us say YES! to life, that lift us up, and inspire us to keep growing.

This is such a crucial point that it bears repeating:

The universe always without exception gives us what we focus on. In can only give us what we want when our motivation is coming from a unified and conscious place. If our way of asking for or imagining our success and fulfillment is at all tied up with subconscious holding patterns, we will be sending out mixed messages. There simply isn't enough clarity in what we are asking for or imagining to bring it into fruition.

When we have relinquished all of the hidden crevasses of our minds that promote internal conflict, we are now free to harness the power of our imagination in a unified way that can bring to fruition a life of purpose and abundance. We do this through the asking of brand new questions that awaken the most animated and alive aspects of who we are. When we embark on this process, the advice of Rainer Maria Rilke in Letters to a Young Poet eloquently summarizes the message of this lesson:

Be patient toward all that is unsolved in your heart and try to love the questions themselves like locked rooms and like books that are written in a very foreign tongue. Do not now seek the answers, which cannot be given you because you would not be able to live them. And the point is, to live everything. Live the questions now. Perhaps you will find them gradually, without noticing it, and live along some distant day into the answer.

A PERSONAL STORY

A perfect example of this is the book you are now reading. Since I was 18 years old, I have imagined myself being an author. Writing was one of the only things I could see myself doing. In fact, I felt a strong desire to write my first book by the time I was 19. I could see it so clearly in my mind. My imagination conjured up crystal clear images and feelings of holding my first book in my hands before I was 20.

I knew that I was most interested in writing about Eastern spirituality. I wanted to share what I was learning with the rest of the Western world. Since much of what I was learning was the only source of help that I could find, I felt a calling to share these insights with others. The problem was that I was going through a period of profound stagnation and depression in my life in which I could not offer much of myself. I could see myself writing, but the questions I asked of myself blocked me from taking action:

- What is wrong with me?
- Why can't I just channel this desire in the right way?
- Why do I feel so stuck?

By attaching to questions such as these, my small self blocked me from the compelling visions my imagination was creating that offered glimpses of my ultimate purpose. I was very problem-oriented.

Interestingly, even as I write this book now there is still that small self trying to chime in with its self-defeating questions such as, "Will I ever get this done?" Even though this still arises, I can cultivate space around it now. Simply shedding awareness on the small self's voice causes it to shrivel up rather quickly and keeps me tuned into my imagination, which has always known that this book would be written, even if it is 15 years after I told myself it would happen!

QUESTIONS THAT AWAKEN PURPOSE

When we ask questions such as the following ones, it is not important that we focus on their immediate answers. Rather, having an open-ended relationship with the questions themselves is, paradoxically, an answer in and of itself. Since these are questions that prompt us to continually evolve and learn, what is important is that we keep asking them so as to remind ourselves of the vastness of our nature and the sacredness of our purpose.

Let's take a look at a few of these questions that we want to focus on in the awakening of our purpose. When considering the best way to give form to your purpose through your job, relationships, lifestyle choices, and finances, it is very helpful to keep returning to these questions.

1 If I take away my name, gender, job title, and any and all conventional roles (husband, teacher, parent, etc.), who am I?

2 If fear and money no longer felt like obstacles in my life, what would I do with my time?

3 What do I love doing more than anything else? What activities fill me with joy, excitement, and meaning?

4 What can I do that will help the most people in this life?

5 What has always come effortlessly to me?

6 If I were to die one week from today, how would I spend my time? What would I say to the people I love? How would I want to be remembered?

7 What force within me can effortlessly enable me to give up any and all addictive behavior?

8 In my heart of hearts, what do I want more than anything else?

9 What are the ways that I have suffered in my life? What are the biggest challenges I have faced? If I were to perceive these events as nothing more than
teachers, what would I have learned? How can I help others based on this?

10 What does my ideal life look like?

USING YOUR IMAGINATION
FOR THE BENEFIT OF OTHERS

These kinds of questions set the stage for reinventing yourself. They shift your
focus completely to a new set of priorities that are based on seizing the importance of this very moment and contributing your very best to the world around
you. They invoke the realizations within you of how you really want to live, of the
things, people, and beliefs that will truly serve the world and enable you to exit it
feeling completely fulfilled and at peace. They take you out of that wounded place
that only knows the problems. They free you up to take your focus off of you and
your problems and bring it to the unique contribution you can make to benefit
others. This is the doorway through which your life purpose is revealed.

If you want to use your imagination to attract the right things and circumstances
to your life, the irony is that *it's far more helpful to imagine other people getting
what they want than it is to focus on yourself and what you want.* Let's look at
an example. Let's say that since you were a child, you have told yourself that you
want a bright red Ferrari more than anything else in the world. You have visual-
ized, felt, and practically tasted that car sitting in your driveway on infinite occasions. Let's stop right here for a moment. Can you see any hint of a problem here?

Your entire focus is on you and what you want.

Your imagination is by far the most effective when you take your focus off of yourself and apply it to the benefit of others. In this case, why not imagine every single person in your neighborhood getting the car of their dreams?

Do you want more money? How about imagining everyone you know achieving their ideal financial life?

Looking for a better love life? Think of other people you know who are even more discouraged about their potential for genuine intimacy and imagine them being deeply fulfilled in a loving relationship.

Wish you were happier? Imagine someone you know who struggles with depression making a drastic change for the better.

You get the picture here.

What this boils down to is the fact that your imagination is ultimately a tool for cultivating generosity and letting go of your small self. Your ideal life can only arise when you let go of self-preoccupation and put your focus on how you can help others, either energetically through your imagination or practically through your actions.

Now, does this mean you will get the Ferrari by imagining everyone you know getting their dream car? Maybe, maybe not. What you'll likely see if you do this exercise on a regular basis is that the things that you want or covet are really just symbols of your attempts at self-generosity. When we want a new Ferrari, more money in the bank, or a better relationship, we are simply trying to figure out how we can be generous with ourselves. When we do this exercise, we are actually arousing the energy of generosity in the most powerful and direct way possible. When we do this, we don't really care if we ever get the Ferrari or not! We are giving to ourselves the real essence of what the Ferrari symbolizes.

Now, let's return for a moment to the problem-oriented questions that we asked at the beginning of this chapter and rephrase them as if our awakened imagination was in charge:

1 *Problem-oriented*: Why am I so fat?

   Solution-oriented: Who is the real me beneath this weight? Where is this being who is so much more than this body, this being of light, freedom, and space? Am I ready to meet that being, possibly for the first time? Can I have compassion for myself for the reasons why I may be carrying extra weight? Can I somehow be of service to others who carry extra weight?

2 *Problem-oriented*: I know I should just bear down and find a way to like my job, but I just can't seem to do it. What the heck is wrong with me?

   Solution-oriented: If I were to identify the most powerful and useful contribution that I could make to this world, if I were to unleash my unique gifts and the qualities that make me shine, does this job allow me to do that? If not, what form do I wish to give my innate attributes so they can be fully expressed to the world? How can I help others who feel stuck in a dead-end job?

3 *Problem-oriented*: I hate this debt. What in the world can I do to make it go away?

   Solution-oriented: Who is this person that has struggled with self-worth and feeling valued? What would happen if I shifted my focus to the person within me who is already financially free? To the person that can make a priceless offering to this world and sees this temporary debt as just another lesson that will enable me to more fully help others? How can I help others who are experiencing financial difficulty?

4 *Problem-oriented*: I just can't stand getting hurt by men anymore. Why don't they want to be with me? Is it because I'm just not that attractive?

Solution-oriented: Who is this person that doesn't trust and feels betrayed? What would happen if, before I allowed myself to be with another man, I would identify with a place of self-love first? What if I shifted my focus from feeling wounded and betrayed to this place within me that is full of love and is already whole? What if I acted as if I am already completely fulfilled and that I don't need a man to make me more complete? How can I help others who feel unfulfilled in their relationships?

5 *Problem-oriented*: How do I make this pain in my body go away?

Solution-oriented: Who is this person who feels so much pain? Is there a place in my Being that is completely unscathed by what my body is experiencing? Can I go to that place and identify with it? Can I then use this pain as a way to help others?

6 *Problem-oriented*: Where in the hell did I put my car keys? I always lose those damn things.

Solution-oriented: What does it say about me that I always lose my car keys? Can I set an intention right now to bring more calmness to my inner reality so I can be more organized in my outer reality?

EXERCISES

1. See if you can identify any problem-oriented questions you ask yourself.

   In case this still isn't clear to you, here are a few more examples of problem-oriented questions:

   - Why won't my kids ever listen to me?

   - Why can't I get my husband to care more about our marriage?

   - Why won't my wife clean this house for once?

   - What can I do to get back at my boss for being such a jerk?

   - If I exercise three hours a day every day, will that take off this [expletive] weight?

   - My life feels boring. What can I do to occupy my time better?

   - I want a new house but I can't afford it. Why can't I make more money?

   - This anxiety is out of control. Do you think that new medication I saw on TV will take care of the problem?

Hopefully you are starting to see what problem-oriented questions look like. Now, just as we did at the end of the chapter, look at the questions you ask on a regular basis and see if you can turn them around through the power of your imagination to be solution-oriented.

Okay, let's answer some questions.

Sometimes I feel like my imagination can get me in trouble. It can steer me down the wrong path. I end up pursuing things that really aren't that feasible. What do I do about this?

An integral part of using imagination to our benefit is discerning when we are caught in wishful thinking and when we are truly sparked by a vision for what we want, which is grounded in who we really are. Wishful thinking is yet another form of self-deception and resistance that prevents us from making authentic change. It is steeped in mere fantasy and is not at all aligned with our real purpose. This harkens back to the point that we have to know ourselves intimately enough to know what we really want and what kinds of questions to ask the universe.

Purpose always carries with it a high degree of personal accountability. If we were the sole provider for our family, it would be irresponsible to suddenly quit our job to pursue our fantasy of being the lead singer in a rock and roll band. It would be irresponsible to abandon our family to pursue a new romance that we have fantasized about. The power of imagination does not give us entitlement to fall victim to the whims of temptation. If we are doing harm to others, then we are off track. This is a simple yet important guideline to follow as we learn how to utilize our imagination to our ultimate benefit.

When we use our imagination in the right way, is this the same thing as positive thinking?

Not exactly. Many of us have read various self-improvement or success books that preach the importance of positive thinking as the best way to secure success in our lives. The problem is that we can engage in the practice of positive thinking without actually doing a thing about all of the subconscious holding patterns that are undermining our life experience. Just because we are manufacturing and repeating positive statements to ourselves does not mean that the intensity behind our deeper beliefs is being lessened. This is why so many of us are disappointed by the lack of results we get from positive thinking.

When we invoke the power of imagination, we are tapping into the infinite space of our being that is beyond what we think and feel. If our main reference point for changing ourselves is our thoughts, we are still dwelling in the territory of the small self that can easily sabotage our efforts. Thoughts arise as a by-product of our belief systems. We tend to think negative thoughts when the beliefs that underlie them are likewise negative. Rather than tampering with the tone of our thoughts, a more direct way to freedom is to expose the beliefs that underlie our thoughts and then shift our focus to the space around them. If we try to change our negative thoughts to positive ones, we will often find that there is a quality of force that feels unnatural or contrived.

It is important to note that our thoughts do play a vital role in the outer reality that we currently have. If we think about something on a regular basis, it tends to show up in our outer circumstances. The key here is to allow the change from negative to positive thoughts to be a natural by-product of doing the deeper work of freeing ourselves of limiting beliefs and perceptions, and keeping our focus in a place of nonresistance and spaciousness. When we do this, our thoughts naturally become more life-affirming and positive.

Many people get stuck in trying to be more positive, healthy, or successful without tapping into the deeper source that enables these conditions to be actualized. We can't just manufacture feelings of positivity when we are out of alignment with our purpose. We must go to the source of purpose first, then allow the shift to a higher, more positive state of mind to arise in a natural way.

I have also heard that I need to feel good before I can have what I want in my life. How does this fit into this discussion?

Once again, instead of trying to manufacture a positive feeling, go to that place within yourself that is beyond what you think and feel. There is a source of ultimate well-being that resides in each of us that is beyond our conditioned emotions and feelings. It is always there, regardless of our temporary states of mind. When we talk about feeling good, it is more an impersonal feeling of tapping into infinite space rather than contriving some temporary feeling of positivity in order to create the life you want.

The teaching we should "feel good" as a way to get what we want is an oversimplified and inaccessible suggestion to so many of us. If we knew how to turn on the "feel good" switch, we would have done that already. Instead of starting out with a focus on feeling good, start by recognizing the power of your purpose and affirming that you are ready to live in accordance with it. When you have cleared all of your obstacles to living this way, then a feeling of goodness will naturally arise. It is a by-product of doing the deeper work and cannot be forced into being. You will then see that you can access purpose even if you aren't feeling good. It is available in every moment.

Now, let's move on to the seventh strategy, which is all about consistency and repetition.

Commit to Your Purpose at All Times

When you feel in your gut what you are and then dynamically pursue it—don't back down and don't give up—then you're going to mystify a lot of folks.

—Bob Dylan

The school of real life will test you every day to see how committed you are to your true purpose. This strategy will help you to pass these tests so you can keep growing toward greater states of freedom and wellness.

At this point, you have initiated the process of awakening to your real purpose in life. You have declared that your purpose is more important than anything else; you have uncovered your own obstacles to purpose; you have given these obstacles some space so you can embark on the process of change in a refreshingly new way; and you have tapped into the astonishing power of your imagination as an ally in uncovering your reason for being.

All of these steps are essential for launching a new you into reality. They give you powerful snapshots of how amazing your life can be when all of that wonderful potential you have is brought out into the world. This next step is about sustaining the realization of purpose consistently, day in and day out for as long as you live. This step is the antidote to another common stumbling block: recognizing your purpose but then getting sucked back into old ways of being that keep it suppressed. While it is wonderful and crucial to have these initial flickers of insight into who we really are, they will only serve us if we make a commitment to the constant presence of our purpose regardless of what happens to us in life.

REPETITION IS KEY!

There are indeed many people who have had a spiritual opening, some sort of deep insight that caused a transformation to take place. At first, it can feel earth-shattering. We feel like we are born anew into a world we have never known. However, the power of our old ways of being can be incredibly seductive and can insidiously drag us back to the comfortable reference points that previously pro-moted feelings of mediocrity, anger, depression, or boredom. Many of us become convinced after an initial opening that our newfound realization will create its own momentum and we can now passively partake in all of the glory that has been revealed to us for as long as we live. This is rarely the case. It takes a com-mitment to ourselves to sustain and cultivate our temporary openings so that they do indeed become the norm of our experience rather than some anomalous occurrence that ultimately has little impact on our daily life.

This strategy is basically saying we have to have a daily relationship with the third strategy, putting our purpose first, every day that we live. Whether we have had an awakening or we feel mired down in old baggage, we are still committed to our purpose beyond all else. In this sense, whatever life brings to us, we use it as an opportunity to wake up and open our hearts. What we used to interpret as bad, negative, or unwanted, we now use as a catalyst for the evolution of our purpose. In this way, we transform our deepest pains into our greatest virtues. By doing this, we are basically resting our attention in the place within us that is stronger than anything that can happen to us from the outside. We are commit-ting to make that initial 1% flicker of purpose (that we talked about in the fifth strategy) the predominant foundation of our being.

Do you remember the examples we used in that fifth strategy of the person stuck in traffic and the mom whose child was grating on her all day long? They each experienced a temporary opening when they focused on the space around the situation. The odds are very high, however, that each of them would experience virtually identical situations in the very near future and they would have to choose how purposeful their response would be. As the late driver realizes yet again that he's stuck in traffic for the umpteenth time, he can either expand or contract. The more he expands by being aware of the dynamics of that moment, the more he is planting the seed to activate his innate gifts, awaken his heartfelt aspirations, and fulfill his limitless potential.

And what are the odds that the parent would have to face a crying baby again? As space is repeatedly brought to that situation, the parent would be offering their child (and themselves) the most precious gift of all, which is pure awareness or presence. No resistance.

Every one of us can draw on this infinite source of strength from within our own Being. It is our Spirit, our essence that has never been and can never be damaged or hurt by anything that happens to us in this life. It is the ultimate refuge when life feels unworkable. When we make a commitment to identify with this inner wisdom, we are asserting our deepest belief that the universe is ultimately a benevolent and positive place. Why do we believe this? *Because this essence is untouched by life experience. It is steeped in the ground of Being, the place of complete stillness where nothing ever happens.*

Making this commitment to our purpose shows us with increasing clarity that our suffering is caused by how we interpret life and what we believe to be true about it, not life experience in and of itself. This is the most direct path we can take out of a substandard, victim-based life. It puts us in the driver's seat by giving us a direct experience of the limitless openness of the universe we are part of.

OUR COMMITMENT WILL BE TESTED EVERY DAY

The reason it's important to spend some time on this subject is that the universe has a way of dredging up each and every obstacle we have created so we can move through it. At every point along the way, we get to choose if we are going to use our life experience to wake up and keep growing or as further evidence to confirm our harmful beliefs and storylines. When we commit to our purpose, we are choosing to use every input from life as a way to keep moving forward. We simply don't allow ourselves to get stuck in old, habitual perceptions. As we keep peeling away the layers of our armoring, the universe can increase the intensity of the situations that come to us. We are put into situations that can make us feel destabilized and confused, or like we want to recoil into our old self. As the intensity increases, our commitment to our purpose must also increase.

If our commitment plateaus or starts to wane, then the challenges presented to us will feel unworkable. We will get dragged down and lose our sacred perspective. We will allow more doubt into our life. "Maybe all of this is just a crock," we'll think to ourselves. "Maybe I should have just kept going along as I was before. It really wasn't that bad, after all."

When this voice creeps in, it's important to bring the fifth strategy into the equation. Recognize that doubt has crept into your life and bring a lot of space to it. Have gratitude that you can see it for what it is without getting attached to it. You simply notice, "Oh, interesting. Doubt is showing up." No attachment, no resistance. You simply acknowledge it and then put your focus back on who you really are and the life you really want to live.

This is the sacred dance of life that keeps us in a state of constant evolution. Attachment and resistance are the forces that cause us to regress and stagnate. We get stuck in our current state of mind or our current circumstances, then we feed it by trying to make the perceived discomfort go away or force something better into our lives. Every day, we get to choose: Will we bring space and ease of being to our current reality? Will we return to our deeper purpose and put our focus there? This dance never stops. We continually engage with it every day that we live. If we think that we have finally gotten it, that we can now go on autopilot, we will soon find that we have become stuck, that anger or other difficult emotions are arising within us.

A NEW WAY OF WORKING WITH SUFFERING: TRANSFORMING IT INTO ITS OPPOSITE

Turn your wounds into wisdom.

—Oprah Winfrey

Transmuting pain into virtue is not something that most of us are taught growing up. It may sound like a very foreign concept and it may feel awkward as you practice this in your life. Keep in mind that this is indeed a practice. It's okay if it feels foreign to you at first. In many other cultures, this attitude toward life is taught at a very young age. It is nurtured in children and accepted as the best way to live into adulthood. In our society, however, there is a deep strain of conditioning that suggests we should use will power and black-and-white thinking to get through life. We get trapped in the dualism of good/bad, success/failure, and so on. Bringing space to our life experience is about allowing such tendencies to polarize life to be there without attachment. In this way, we will never get stuck because we will see every event that happens in life, good or bad, as a lesson that we can grow from.

It's important to clarify here that transmuting our pain into virtue in no way minimizes or negates the suffering we feel when tragedy strikes or when life throws us a curveball. Committing to our purpose does not mean that we will never feel pain again. In fact, we become vastly more open to the suffering around us. The key point here is that we no longer use tragedy or hardship as an excuse for our life to shut down. We don't internalize or identify with suffering. Instead, we use it as a way to open ourselves more and bring out our very best. In this way, there is a world of difference between being open to helping others who are suffering versus being enslaved by our own personal suffering.

CASE STUDY ☙ **AMANDA** ☙

Amanda came to my practice after struggling for years with a clinically diagnosed case of hypothyroidism. This had resulted from many years spent juggling her roles as a mom to her two children and her very demanding job managing a number of employees in a healthcare clinic. Although Amanda had given up that job several years ago and her children were now grown up, she was still suffering from the residual effects of spending most of her adult life working too hard and not resting enough.

After working with Amanda over the course of a few weeks, it became apparent that the real source of her fatigue was her habitual tendency to overextend herself and to ingratiate others at her own expense. In particular, a few of her family members were particularly draining, as they regularly expected her to conform to their expectations and demands without sensitivity to her own needs.

Amanda was operating under the false belief that she had to give of herself unconditionally in order to be a good person. Because of her attachment to this belief, she did not know how to set healthy boundaries, which repeatedly put her in situations that drained her. Amanda was truly ready to put her purpose first, which really came down to putting her own authentic needs first so she could consolidate her energy in order to heal her thyroid condition.

Based on her newfound desire to live with purpose, she took a stand with her family members by mindfully telling them that she was no longer

continued

willing to oblige their demands of her. The real test came as she experienced quite a backlash from her family, as they took a "how dare you" stance with her. While this would have previously made Amanda feel guilty or like she was the one to blame, she committed to her purpose and stood her ground. For the most part, she cut her ties with all of the people in her life who had previously drained her. Even though her family could not understand her choice to do so, Amanda knew in her bones that she was on track with her purpose.

In order to commit to her purpose, Amanda also had to train herself to see the merit in resting. She had learned from an early age that resting is a sign of laziness and that she had to work constantly in order to be deemed successful. In the initial phases, it was actually a discipline for her to devote large segments of her time to doing nothing, focusing on her own needs, and spiritually and physically rejuvenating herself. It actually took a strong commitment to stay with this, as she was deeply programmed to do the exact opposite.

After a few weeks of working with Amanda, the change was drastic. She was emotionally lighter, had way more energy, and exuded a quiet confidence that came from an inner knowing that she was aligned with purpose. She was even able to wean off of her thyroid medication, which her Western doctors told her would never happen.

All too often, our society makes the assumption that finding purpose means feeling good. But when we choose to live in accordance with what is true, as Amanda did, our purpose isn't just about feeling better. It is about going directly into the obstacles to purpose and then committing to the truth no matter what. This can be very painful at first, as Amanda experienced in having to confront her family and the backlash she received from them. Ultimately, this brought her to a much higher state of wellness and freedom, but it required a deep commitment on her part to persevere.

In the context of life purpose we have discussed to this point, we could say that faith is what enables us to make this commitment to the life that we really want, even in the face of hardship or when there is a gap between the focus of our intention and its actual manifestation into reality. It takes faith to perceive everything that happens to us as an opportunity to learn and evolve and to stay committed to what we really want, even when it doesn't show up immediately. Faith comes not just from a belief in a deeper potential within us, but an inner knowing that this potential is the basis of who we are. Even when we experience doubt, fear, or adversity, we can always return to a place of inner stillness that is alive with our sacred purpose. Faith is the recognition we have of this place and its capacity to bring us what we need to continue moving forward.

We all know that life can feel like a messy affair that does not typically conform to our expectations of how things should be. Faith is the knowledge we have that the universe brings us exactly what we need in order to evolve—nothing more and nothing less. This is the case even when we don't understand the message or lesson we're receiving. Even when we experience confusion or insecurity, we can still have faith that, so long as we're committed to it, our deeper purpose is always setting the stage for creating the exact situations we need to learn from.

This seventh strategy is about the perseverance that arises due to the faith we have in ourselves and in the goodness of the universe. Genuine perseverance arises automatically when we know who we really are and what our mission is. No matter what happens, we keep committing to our purpose because that is what we are here to do. This kind of perseverance creates a feeling of unshakable confidence that we are stronger than anything that happens to us. It is the basis of invincible power. What an incredible realization it is to know that we are unstoppable!

THE VIRTUE OF QUITTING

The kind of perseverance we are discussing here is not at all based on asserting our iron will on to the world and forcing life to acquiesce to what we think we want.

In this sense, one of the highest virtues is knowing when to quit. Indeed, declaring our purpose before all else can often mean that we have to completely sever our ties with projects, relationships, or careers that we have tried so hard to make work.

The mistake that so many of us make is that we try to jump to this seventh strategy before doing the real work on the previous six strategies. We end up committing to the wrong things, then we wonder why, since our commitment is so strong, things aren't working out as we'd like them to. What we ask for and desire doesn't show up for us and life feels like a struggle to achieve what we think we should achieve. Because of this, we lose faith. We resign ourselves to mediocrity, depression, or underachievement, convincing ourselves that we have tried to live our dreams, but it just didn't happen. Or we beat our heads against the wall year after year, never really allowing in the increasingly stark messages that we are getting (in the form of high blood pressure, alcoholism, overwhelming stress, a tense marriage, horrible insomnia, etc.) that we are simply off track and that we need to abandon our current course of action and pursue something radically different as soon as humanly possible.

This seventh strategy is about staying in a constant state of receptivity so we know if we are on the right track. We need to pay close attention to the validation (or lack thereof) that we are getting from the universe. Sometimes, it can indeed be that we simply need to persevere. We are on target and we are forging ahead with the right commitment. Giving up would be the tragedy of a lifetime. We all know how easy it is to be besieged by fear and doubt. So how do we know if our commitment is coming from the right place?

GETTING IT IN A WHISPER

Committing to your life purpose is based on a moment-to-moment relationship you have with yourself and the universe. In order to stay attuned to your purpose, you must be receptive to the messages you receive from within and without. Have you ever noticed that, on occasion, a little voice or feeling wells up within you that is trying to prompt you in a certain direction? If you try to force a decision without listening to this voice, you will often look back with regret and say, "You know, there was something inside of me that *knew* this was not the right choice. Why didn't I listen to that?"

Other times, something rather symbolic or serendipitous can happen in your life that gives you a sense of guidance or confirmation. We are in constant communication with our environment and the universe at large. We are always sending and receiving signals that help us to navigate our way through life. How skillfully we utilize these signals is primarily determined by how conscious we are of what we are emitting and what we are receiving. We have to be aware of that still, small voice within and what the universe is showing us on a daily basis. This awareness is a practice. Every single strategy you have learned up to this point is priming you for this greater awareness that can keep you in a state of deep receptivity.

What blocks this receptivity? Attachment to speed, doubt, fear, addictions, negativity—all of the mental chatter and lifestyle choices being fueled by the small self. When we identify with the small self in this way, life will always feel random. We will be cut off from our deeper intuition that can guide us through life gracefully. We will feel separate from the universe, so we won't be able to see our circumstances as teachings that are intended to refine our awareness so we can choose a more purposeful and abundant life.

When we can get it in a whisper, our awareness practice is bearing fruit. We will be able to heed subtle signals that something is a bit off or that we need to modify our course. If we don't "get it" on a subtle level, then the universe has a way of offering us increasingly stark messages. If we miss the whisper, then it's like a little rock falls on our head. We say, "Ouch, what was that?" If we continue to remain blind to our purpose, then the next rock that falls is a little bigger, which means that the distress we are feeling or the force we are putting into things is magnified. This process will continue to become more pronounced until we are hit by a metaphorical (or in some cases, a literal) truck. In this case, disaster hits and we have to choose between continuing to relate to the situation with our small self or expand our awareness so we can finally learn the lesson.

Many of us finally come to a place of purpose only after enduring a great deal of suffering, failure, or hardship. Our small self clings to existence so vehemently that it takes something this extremely unsettling and painful to occur in order for us to break free and wake up. Does it have to be this way? Absolutely not. We can choose to get it in a whisper starting right now by being proactive instead of reactive. We can stop putting off what's most important. For many of us, this entails a radical departure from the life we have been living that feeds on drama, crisis, and speed. We will only be able to get it in a whisper when we are thoroughly sick of our attachment to these obstacles.

What I have noticed time and again in my acupuncture practice is that every one of us can logically see that it would be best to live in this way. I have heard countless patients say, "Of course I don't want more stress, depression and drama! Why on earth would I?"

If you have closely followed the previous strategies, you can likely see that there is a huge payoff for staying immersed in dysfunctional emotions and circumstances: It is a surefire way of feeling some semblance of control in life and avoiding the uncertainty and groundlessness of our own nature. This is the only reason why any of us would choose to live with hardship and stress. It takes courage to be willing to step out of this. For many of us, this courage becomes available to us when we literally can't take another round of the same pain, mediocrity, or distress.

RED FLAGS INDICATING THAT YOU'VE STEERED AWAY FROM YOUR PURPOSE

On a practical level, any time you notice that you are consistently immersed in any one of the following states of mind, then consider it a warning sign that you have steered away from purpose and it's time to be receptive to the whisper:

- ⊙ Will power: Feeling like you have to "push" your way to success or happiness. This only leads to exhaustion.

- ⊙ Boredom: A sign of being disconnected from what inspires you.

- ⊙ Joylessness: Sacrificing joy is never worth what you are trying to achieve.

- Distress: This is a negative and toxic form of energy that makes you feel anxious, distraught, worried, angry, or critical. There is good stress in life, called eustress, which is often aligned with purpose. This form of stress is what you feel on the verge of a major breakthrough or when you are working very hard toward a noble and worthy goal. This form of stress is life-enhancing, whereas distress is life-denying.

HOW DO I KNOW IF I'M ON THE RIGHT TRACK?

When we put it out to the universe that we are ready to live with purpose, what happens is that our purpose finds us, we don't find it. What this means is that our life becomes devoted to being and doing only the things that are in alignment with our true nature. We simply cannot do anything but this. For instance, when we consider the kind of work we are meant to be doing, we are left with one clear choice that has been right there in front of us, but there may have been too much fear, resistance, or doubt to allow it to be seen as part of our reality. We go for this kind of work because it is all there is for us to do after we remove all of our agendas and expectations about who we should be. It is the kind of work that resonates with us the most, makes us feel the most excited, and draws out our innate gifts the best. But since we are left with this and this alone, this kind of work chooses us. It has always been there as the clearest form of what we can offer. It's just that now we have finally cleared out the obfuscations so we can see it.

When doubt or fear tries to dissuade us from this choice, we are left with the simple question that keeps us coming back: "But what else would I do?" There is nothing out there that speaks to us in the same way. This kind of understanding is what keeps many successful people moving forward through adversity in order to reach their goals. They have come to a one-pointed place of unity within themselves that knows that they are on the right track, simply because there is absolutely nothing they would rather be spending their time doing.

As you will see in the eighth strategy, you can apply the Purpose Principle to every dimension of life. We are always left with a clear choice of action because that is simply the only light we see in the situation. Whatever has caused you to struggle, your purpose is the only way out. You have exhausted every other option. For instance, if you have experienced a lot of suffering around your weight, you have probably tried just about everything you can think of to lose those extra pounds. You have come to a place of complete exasperation with the whole problem. In this situation, your life purpose is the only clear voice of sanity that can guide you through this perceived problem. When you drop the resistance to the extra weight and stop trying to change yourself out of force, your purpose in this situation arises naturally. You will realize a radically new way of relating to yourself that has nothing to do with the million and one ways you have tried so hard to escape this frustrating cycle. This new way is based on space, love, and acceptance. As you surrender to this new way, you see it is and has always been the only way out of the perceived problem.

This new way is not based on will power, distress, negative emotions, or joylessness. It arises when we surrender and give space to the situation. When we do this, we make contact with this place within us that has no anger toward the extra weight. This place does not perceive the weight as a problem. Instead, all it sees is the opportunity to learn a new lesson and relate to our body in a refreshingly new way that affirms, rather than negates, its existence.

This same kind of opening can be brought to anything in life that feels like a struggle, whether it's our marriage, finances, job, or family life. When we bring space to our life, there is always one clear way out of our struggle that is, in essence, the only way out. This way typically does not lead to immediate gratification or to making everyone around us feel more placated, but it is the most honest choice we can make. As we bring this quality of surrender to life, it can feel awkward at first. Like each strategy we have covered, it is a practice. The more we commit to this kind of relationship with ourselves, the easier it becomes to surrender resistance and choose the best and most authentic way to proceed through life.

Once we start doing this in every dimension of life, the universe has a way of validating our integrity. We will devote a whole upcoming strategy to what life looks like when our life purpose is actualized (refer to the tenth strategy, Become Your Purpose).

While that strategy will go into much more detail, let's just say here that there are many states of mind and signs of universal confirmation that can arise when you are plugged into your purpose. Included in this list are qualities such as joy, contentment, gratitude, connection, ease of being, synchronicity, even miracles. While it is true that being aligned with purpose tends to evoke more positive qualities such as these, it's important not to romanticize this too much.

From the perspective of our Spirit (the place within that is beyond the small self), life purpose is simply what we are here to do. The fact that it stimulates more positive emotions into being is great, but that isn't really what we focus on. It's easy to slip into a way of relating to purpose that is based on the agenda of wanting to feel or be better, as if living with purpose will lead to some sort of prize. The small self can easily turn this into a game of self-aggrandizement where we set up a conditional relationship with our purpose that goes, "I'll commit to being more kind and authentic and to offering myself to others if it makes me feel better, look younger, get more praise, and other 'comforts.'"

Life purpose is unconditional. You commit to it because that is what you are here to do. Sometimes this will feel very challenging and sometimes very wonderful. Whatever you feel about it doesn't really matter. What's important is making this your top priority every day that you're alive. If you look at people who exemplify purposeful living, like Gandhi or Mother Teresa, it is clear that their lives were not always easy. In fact, they faced more challenges and adversity than most of us could even imagine. They kept their commitment to their purpose intact because that is why they showed up here in the first place. That commitment inspired millions of people and changed the world on many levels. On a personal level, however, the sacrifice they went through was immense. There is simply no way they could have devoted their lives to serving others in such a profound way if the small self was at all involved, if there was a separate sense of "I" that was looking for personal validation or reward.

Even though the examples of Gandhi and Mother Teresa may seem like far-removed ideals from where you are right now, it is important to know that you have the same potential to commit to your purpose to create positive change in the world. That is the beauty of going beyond the small self. We see that there is infinite space in what we call "I," our personal identity. There truly is no limit to who we are or the impact we can make when we renew our commitment to purpose every day that we live.

COMMITMENT AND INTENSITY

Perhaps the greatest obstacle we have in maintaining an ongoing commitment to our purpose is the quiet, insidious, and subtle process of gradually settling back into our comfort zone. We find that our initial desire to live with purpose is slowly blanketed by the numbing effects of having lived a certain way for so long. Day by day, we slip back into what we know. We return to our old friends, addictions, and perceptions. We tend to stay in the familiar until, once again, life wakes us up and we become inspired to break free of our habitual ways. Many of us become stuck in this cycle of experiencing momentary glimpses of our infinite potential, only to have it thwarted by the small self that lulls us back into a docile trance.

Does it have to be this way? Certainly not. We can choose to commit to our purpose with more intensity each and every day. The only way to do this, however, is if our desire is strong enough to keep life purpose as THE top priority for each day that we are alive. Nothing can stand in its way. Nothing can quiet it or seduce it to sleep. We learn to use time as our ally in the sense that the longer we are alive, the more developed and conscious our purpose becomes. Without a compelling reason to maintain the commitment, however, time can gradually work against us and lull us back to sleep. We will forget.

How do we keep the desire for purpose high?

1 By seeing with absolute clarity what happens to us when we live in any other way. We have to be diligent about maintaining an awareness of what we really want, or else the comfortable hum of our old way of being will find its way back into our reality.

2 By feeding off of the inspiration we feel and offer to others. When we taste this wonderful gift, we become intent on deepening and expanding its presence in our lives.

Waking up is the process of maintaining an intense focus on the life that we want to live, even if our small self finds it to be uncomfortable, ungratifying, or even downright repulsive. We have crystal clear awareness about what the small self has to offer and we are simply no longer interested. This is how we maintain the intensity for purpose day in and day out. Eventually, this intensity for life becomes our natural way of being in the world. As we stabilize ourselves in our purpose, however, we need to set strong intentions to stay awake each and every day. We have to see when the small self is sneaking in to try and undermine our evolution. Remember, any time we notice that we're experiencing the red flags mentioned in this lesson, we're missing our purpose. In those instances, we're using excessive will power; we feel a lot of distress; we're bound up in negative states of mind like doubt, fear, and anger; we don't have much joy; or we feel bored and uninspired.

EXERCISES

1 Make it a practice to begin each and every day by declaring that you are ready to put your purpose first.

2 Practice cultivating intensity for life. This doesn't mean that you allow in feelings of urgency or anxiety. It means that you bring yourself to a one-pointed focus on this present moment. When you do this, you feel the enormity of yourself and the world you live in. You no longer see life through the lens of the small self that makes things look dull, rote, or familiar.

You have now learned the foundation

of the Purpose Principle.

REPETITION IS KEY! LET'S REVIEW THIS FOUNDATION, FOR IF YOU CAN MAKE IT SECOND NATURE, THEN THE APPLICATION BECOMES EFFORTLESS

1 Whether you realize it or not, you have a sacred purpose for being here.

2 Life purpose begins with the quality of your being, with how you are relating to this moment, and then extends out to what you do.

3 Your current reality has arisen due to the beliefs, values, and feelings that you have carried within you since childhood. Much of what we have learned from external influences from the time we were born has obscured us from our deeper purpose.

4 Unless you proactively choose a life of purpose, you will carry out the momentum of these beliefs until the day you die.

5 When you declare the importance of your purpose, you are essentially saying that you want to be completely free of any limiting conditioning that you have absorbed since day one.

6 To be free, you cannot try to change yourself with the same motivation and understanding that created your problems in the first place. You must contact a new resource of wisdom within yourself.

7 This new resource begins with cultivating space around our current reality. In this way, you no longer resist your current situation.

8 Dropping the resistance creates a new kind of openness that enables you to attract a new reality into your life.

9 When you embark on this process, you feel tremendous gratitude for your willingness to do this, for the limitless potential of each moment, and even for the trauma and pain you have felt up to this point.

10 As you free yourself of the obstacles to purpose, you become better able to use your awakened imagination to clarify who you really are and what you really want.

11 Awakened imagination is the gateway to your deeper purpose, which enables you to access and express your innate gifts, heartfelt aspirations, and limitless potential.

12 Once you have a glimpse into this way of living, the next step is to commit to this process each and every day.

You now have a new foundation upon which to build your life. Now let's take this foundation and apply it to all of the main life themes in section II.

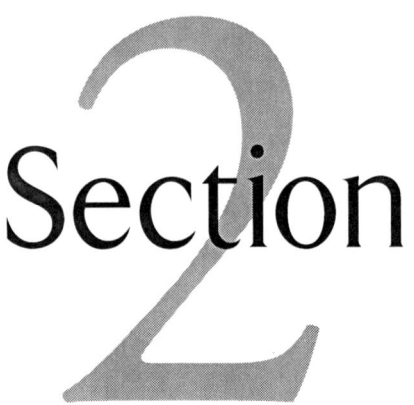

Section 2

THE APPLICATION
of the
Purpose Principle

You have already gotten a taste for how the foundation of the Purpose Principle relates to various areas of life such as money, parenting, health, and relationships. In this section, beginning with the eighth strategy, we will explore in greater depth how you can apply the Purpose Principle to these major life themes.

Don't forget, while it's crucial to learn about and understand this foundation, by far the most important step is actually implementing it into the fabric of your daily life. Section II will ground a lot of the information you have learned so you can see with increasing clarity how to act upon these strategies. The best thing you can do at this point is to make a commitment to acting upon what you have learned.

To further enhance your understanding, a number of practical suggestions and techniques will be discussed in the ninth strategy.

Remember, your practice is to experience your life as an ongoing and constant opportunity to apply this foundation. Regardless of what is happening in your life at any given time, whether it feels good or bad, always return to the Purpose Principle.

Use the Purpose Principle to Go from Basic Survival to Boundless Generosity and Freedom

WORK, MONEY, LOVE, HEALTH, AND PARENTING

How you do anything is how you do everything.

—Harv Eker

The first seven strategies you've learned up to this point are meant to be integrated into all aspects of your daily life. When we realize that our purpose always begins with our inner being, we see that the whole point is to infuse our entire life with purpose. The above quote by Harv Eker brilliantly suggests that we can't cultivate freedom in one area of life to the exclusion of another. For instance, we can't bring 110% of our energy and ambition to our job without giving much attention at all to our health or marriage. Likewise, we can't cultivate a high degree of physical and emotional health if our financial life is neglected. Every piece of the puzzle functions interdependently. If we exclude one piece from our care and attention, then whatever we do focus on will be undermined.

THE UNIFYING THREAD THOUGH EVERY LIFE THEME

Our modern Western culture is reductionistic in nature, which means that we treat the various phenomena of life as isolated entities. When we focus on one thing, such as our job, we often treat it as if it's separate from other factors, such as our health. When we do this, we can easily miss the bigger picture. In this sense, we have experts and books that are exclusively devoted to specific areas such as money, health, psychology, and relationships. What we tend to forget, however, is that there is a unifying thread through all of these topics that makes them inextricably connected. This thread is pure awareness, which underlies every moment that we are alive. If we aren't focused on the underlying awareness behind money or work or health, we can never really get to the core influence that determines how well everything functions and flows.

If our main focus is on awareness itself instead of these seemingly separate life issues, then our outer life tends to be cohesive and unified. We bring a heightened quality of Being to every moment, whether that moment emphasizes our love life, work, money, or dietary choices.

Let's take a look at a few of the main life themes and how to create this cohesion and unity by utilizing our purpose in relation to each of them. Indeed, this is the missing link for so many of us. When we bring purpose and awareness to each of these themes, we will find that we can shed a new light on every aspect of life, a light that is based on knowing ourselves from applying the Purpose Principle. Instead of spinning our wheels trying to find the right relationship or the magic bullet that will enable us to lose 20 pounds only to end up in the same frustrating place over and over, we bring this refreshing and profound quality of spacious awareness to each issue. We set an intention to cut through the habitual and addictive tendencies that cause us to attract the same reality again and again.

This is the secret key to creating a life of optimum wellness and freedom. After all, everything that is showing up in outer reality is just a reflection of what we believe to be true about who we are and how life is. If we focus exclusively on our outer reality, then we will inevitably find ourselves fighting against it. We will be mired in resistance. On the other hand, when we go against convention and plunge into our inner reality (thoughts, beliefs, emotions, and perceptions), then we realize that we have an amazing ability to change our outer circumstances simply by creating space around the small self and expanding into our purpose-based Self.

Whatever theme in your life appears to be a source of distress, know that you can create a radical shift in this moment. It always begins with applying the Purpose Principle right here, right now.

THE PURPOSE PRINCIPLE AND WORK

Work is love made visible. And if you cannot work with love but only with distaste, it is better you should leave your work and sit at the gate of the temple and take alms of those who work with joy.

—Kahlil Gibran

Let's begin this section by applying the Purpose Principle to work. To do this, it is helpful to return to our second definition of life purpose:

> *The identification and expression of our innate gifts, heartfelt aspirations, and limitless potential.*

The kind of work you choose is entirely reflective of the extent to which you have been able to acknowledge and implement this pivotal aspect of your purpose. In this context, we are not just talking about your career or livelihood. This is your primary role in life, whether it's as a stay-at-home mom, firefighter, librarian, retired banker, or high school student. Whatever stage you are at in life and whatever your responsibilities are, you can either live in accordance with this definition of life purpose or you can deny it. This fundamental choice will serve as one of the most important inputs into your overall health and quality of life.

First and foremost, you have to know that you have innate gifts, heartfelt aspirations, and limitless potential. This kind of knowing often surfaces after being stuck in a dead-end job or role for some time and getting hit with the instinctual sense that you are capable of so much more, that you have capacities that far exceed your current job description. When you are ready, you will arrive at a place of knowing and owning your core strengths; you will feel a desire to offer something meaningful and useful based on those strengths; and you will see how the unfolding of this process is a gateway out of the home of the small self and into a much bigger playing field.

You can experience this kind of knowing right now. Start by turning your awareness inward and simply paying closer attention to how you perceive your role in life. This process always begins by looking inward. You have to know that the solution isn't found in a new job or role in life. It is found in your own consciousness.

As you make this fundamental shift toward the "inner solution," you can now declare that you are indeed ready to put your purpose first, to create the most powerful and authentic form possible for your unique gifts, aspirations, and potential. Even if you don't know what this is yet, you are simply clarifying that you are deeply interested in this and that it is a top priority in your life.

Now, let's be sure to emphasize the critical importance of putting your purpose first in relation to your work. Can you see what a vital step this is? You are coming face to face with the truth that you MUST give your purpose the proper form in order to experience any kind of real peace, harmony, or wellness on this planet. You MUST not only access, but express your gifts, aspirations, and potential to the world. It is the only way to freedom. You are not here to settle for less than this, even though a lot of people you know may seem fine going through life without even thinking about these issues. You have a sacred role to fulfill during your time here, which takes precedence over anything else.

Even if it feels scary or uncertain, you remain adamant about creating the perfect form for your purpose. As you do this, you may even hear the voices of your parents or your teachers saying, "No matter what, get a stable, good-paying job with benefits." You will basically come face to face with every internal obstacle that has prevented you from discovering truly purposeful work. Let's take a look at a few other possible blocks:

- The belief that you can't have your cake and eat it too (soul-satisfying work and plenty of money)
- The belief that, whatever role you create, its success will always be determined by hard work and pushing your way to the top
- A cynical feeling that you can't actualize your dreams in the "real world"
- Fear of change, uncertainty, or self-reliance
- A feeling of guilt that you are pursuing your dreams when so many others can't or don't

There are many obstacles to creating purposeful work. What's important is that you honestly assess what is blocking you from your ideal livelihood. As these blocks arise, focus on the space that surrounds them. Can you simply be present to all of the fear, beliefs, negative emotions, addictions, and lifestyle patterns that perpetuate the disconnection from your true calling? Do this without judging or trying to change any of this. Simply let it be and create some separation from these obstacles so you don't identify with them as "me" anymore. Remember, allow no resistance to what is showing up right now, whether it's your inner obstacles or your outer circumstances.

When you do this, you can now utilize the power of your mind in a spontaneous and lucid way. Go back to the purpose-based questions at the end of the sixth strategy and spend some time imagining your ideal work situation or life role. Get to know the details of your core virtues and strengths as a human being, free from all of the "shoulds" and labels that have been put on to you. Arouse the desire you feel to make a mark on the world, to make the most profound contribution possible. Get very clear about this as if it were here with you already—because, ultimately, it actually is here with you.

Lastly, commit to this newfound understanding of your role in life all of the time, even if it doesn't show up in your outer circumstances immediately. Make this the backbone of your daily life. When you do this, you are creating an entirely new inner reality that is steeped in the deepest part of your nature as a human being. Identifying with this reality consistently will guide you to a new set of circumstances and opportunities. This can happen very quickly or it can take some time depending on the clarity and intensity of your identification with your purpose.

Using this blueprint of the Purpose Principle is the most effective, lasting, and genuine solution to creating meaningful work in your life. Now, let's discuss the life theme that is inseparable from the choices you have made in your work: money.

THE PURPOSE PRINCIPLE AND MONEY

Many people desire wealth, but few know how to give it away.

—Francois de La Rochefoucauld

What does it mean to apply the Purpose Principle to the topic of money?

Well, the first thing you'd want to clarify is the purpose that money serves in your life. Do you see it as a problem that you have to put up with, or as a means of taking care of and providing for yourself and those you love? Does your general perception of money reflect lack or fulfillment?

Remember, the objective here is to see every life theme as filling a sacred role in your life. When it comes to money, what would a sacred perception of its purpose in your life look like? Really, the only way that money can be perceived as a symbol of sacredness is when its presence reinforces these three themes:

1 *Survival*—For most of us, our perception of money begins and ends here. We view money as a necessary tool for getting through life. We know that we have to make enough money to get by. Money serves the purpose of taking care of our basic needs and ensuring our protection. Because of this, it becomes a source of self-contraction. We forget to realize that our participation in the daily exchange of money is really a process of helping countless others survive. By perceiving money in a sacred manner, we are essentially recognizing that everyday activities such as paying the bills, buying groceries, or getting a friend a birthday present are opportunities to value ourselves and others, and to value the role money has in our lives. By doing this, we set the stage for the second theme.

2 *Generosity*—If you don't currently perceive money as a symbol of generosity, then it's fruitless to try and make more of it, get out of debt, or somehow escape your financial responsibilities. Our everyday monetary exchanges give us endless opportunities to practice generosity. This doesn't mean that you give all your money to charities. Instead, think of it in a more subtle way. What is going on inside of you as you're handing money to the grocery clerk for your food? Bringing a sacred purpose to money would mean that as you hand that money to the clerk, you would have an understanding of the interconnectedness between you and them. You are both there to serve one another. That person is playing an important role in your life in that moment. Because of this, you would be cheerful toward them and acknowledge their basic goodness as a human being. This is an example of a monetary exchange that energetically conveys generosity. Every exchange with money, whether you receive it or give it, is an opportunity to cultivate this kind of openness.

3 *Freedom*—When we are truly generous in relation to money, we are financially free. This has nothing to do at all with how much money you make or have. Instead, it is the perception you have of money as fulfilling a sacred purpose in your life. Money is a symbol for giving to both yourself and others (yes, it is purposeful to give to yourself). Freedom ultimately comes down to nonattachment, and there is no greater gauge for how attached we are than money. True freedom is an unconditional situation, which means that it is not dependent on external circumstances. As you go through life, it's likely that you'll go through phases where you have a lot of money and can use it to gain wonderful life experiences and help others in need. Other times, you won't have very much money. Either way, you are fundamentally okay. Why? Because you're not attached. The truth is that you are born, you get old, and then you die.

Having a lot of money can't prevent this from happening. It is so easy to buy into the conditioning that you can only live with purpose when you finally have enough money. True fullness, however, comes from within. It comes from recognizing the sacredness of this moment. Whether you have money or not, this moment is still sacred. When you fully absorb this truth, then you are free.

For the time being, stop trying to "do" anything in relation to money and instead turn your attention inward. As you focus on your inner awareness, see if you can choose to perceive money as a symbol of generosity and freedom rather than scarcity and contraction. Focus on the purpose-based Self that is willing to see money in a new light. Starting right now, declare for yourself that, regardless of your current financial state, money is a source of freedom and generosity in your life.

As you do this, it will become clear what your money blocks are. You'll see the subconscious holding patterns coming to the surface that have likely kept you locked in your current financial state year after year. What obstacles do you see? Fear? Perhaps the belief that you're not good enough to have more money? Maybe you feel a lot of frustration with your current financial situation. Here are a few other common obstacles to bringing a sacred purpose to money:

- You spend money unconsciously and habitually
- You are too frugal or cheap—you hoard money
- You wish you could be more generous, but don't know how given that you don't make much money
- You use money as an excuse to put off what really matters to you in your life
- You turn to sweets, alcohol, or other vices when you feel money stress coming on

⊡ You judge other people for having money and put out an unconscious energy of hostility toward them

Whatever obstacles you see, can you bring space to them in this moment? Can you cut through the momentum of the fear, negative beliefs, harmful emotions, or addictions? Can you settle into a quiet acceptance of money in your life as it currently stands? Let the resistance to the presence of money in your life completely fade away.

As you do this, now go deep into your awakened imagination that is free of the obstacles and habits around money. Imagine that money is a symbol of generosity and freedom. Imagine everyone you know having more than enough money and feeling completely liberated by its presence in their lives. Imagine that money fulfills the needs and dreams of countless people on this planet. Imagine that money is a gateway to the full expression of your unique contribution to this planet. Your basic needs are met and you can meet the needs of countless other people.

Now, commit to this newfound understanding of the purpose that money has in your life at all times. Do this even if you are having financial troubles or you feel stressed out about money.

Do you see how the foundation of the Purpose Principle applies to your financial life? You simply can't make positive and authentic outer changes in your finances until you become aware of your inner world and then change it.

Brian came to my acupuncture practice complaining of severe stress, regular outbursts of anger and irritability, and a variety of physical health concerns ranging from poor sleep to heartburn. After asking Brian what was causing so much stress, he described in painful detail how he had built a fairly successful insurance business over the past several years that had left him without one iota of true fulfillment or joy. In fact, he had gotten to the point where he hated his job. He knew it just wasn't a good match for his real interests. He felt imprisoned by his career choice and was only sticking with it for the financial payoff. Unfortunately, this was to the great sacrifice of every other aspect of his life, most notably his health.

Through intensive life coaching and acupuncture sessions and a daily practice of meditation, Brian started to come to terms with how his belief system had landed him in a career that was so dissatisfying. He realized that he was deeply taught to fear life and put his security above all else, which was perfectly aligned with his choice to sell insurance. He had been led to believe that hard work mattered more than anything. Because of this, Brian had used a tremendous amount of will power to create a successful insurance business. By putting so much force and energy into his business, his body was slowly shutting down and his nervous system was unable to find the "off" switch that enabled him to restore himself.

Because he was ready to change, Brian was willing to consider alternatives to his situation, even though it provoked a measurable degree of fear within him. He brought a great deal of space to these harmful beliefs and emotions that had undermined his life. He began to ask new questions of himself to consider what other form to give his purpose. Through activating his imagination and arousing dormant faculties within himself, Brian began to realize that his primary purpose was to help people. In fact, what gave him the most joy was helping people to become as fit and healthy as possible. His insurance work had given him very minute glimpses of this kind of gratification, but he knew it wasn't close to his real passion.

As Brian's consciousness shifted toward this new understanding of his role in life, he gathered the courage to take action on these inner changes. He developed an exit strategy for his insurance business and decided to use his business experience and passion to start a women's fitness center. It was amazing to watch how quickly this all came to fruition, as it was only a few months after Brian exposed and cleared his inner obstacles that he was standing proudly in his new fitness center, helping women become more physically fit. This example shows that the universe likes speed. When our inner and outer worlds come together in this way, things can happen very quickly.

As Brian transitioned out of his insurance career and into what he really wanted to do, his emotional and physical health made drastic improvements. All of the nagging symptoms and emotional outbursts that had plagued Brian for so long dissolved almost effortlessly.

*Loving is fine if you've got plenty of time for walking on
stilts at the edge of your mind.*

—Damien Rice

Now we come to the topic that is more emotionally charged, messy,

dramatic, beautiful, and contradictory than any other: finding and cultivating

true love. Actually, applying the Purpose Principle to your love life is ironically

a pretty straightforward process. Let's begin with the first part of the foundation:

clarifying the sacred purpose of human relationships.

All intimate relationships serve one primary purpose: to mirror back to us the

degree to which we know ourselves. The partner we choose or attract is always

a reflection of how much love, respect, value, and purpose we have developed in

our own life. How intimate each person is with their purpose-based Self is the

core determinant of the health of any relationship. If both people are intimate

with their innermost Being instead of just the small self, then the relationship

has infinite potential for beauty and depth.

The extent to which you can be in a loving relationship is primarily dependent

upon the extent to which you can view the world through the lens of love.

Are you capable of giving and receiving love? Do you know yourself intimately

enough to be able to offer true love to someone else, much less receive it? You

will always attract a partner that reflects back to you how capable you are of

giving and receiving love. That person will either serve as a block or as a gateway

to a deeper expression of love and intimacy depending on how blocked or open

you are to these qualities.

Therefore, the sacred purpose of an intimate relationship is to:

- Give each person a fertile ground and means of connection to know their own nature through the love of another.
- Find someone who can complement your own process of self-discovery in an empowering and supportive way. That person can actually help you to access and express your innate gifts, aspirations, and potential rather than undermining your purpose.
- Strike a balance between spiritual/emotional intimacy and chemistry/passion. If you have too much passion without spiritual and emotional intimacy, then the relationship is bound to be replete with drama, conflict, or fighting. If, on the other hand, there is spiritual and emotional intimacy without passion, then the relationship is destined for a kind of flatness that would make one question whether it's a loving relationship or just a friendship.

After some time in a relationship, no matter how great the other person is, it is inevitable that the way you relate to your partner directly reflects how you relate to yourself. If you value yourself, then it's likely you'll find a partner who will complement and reflect this back to you. If you go into the relationship to seek validation from your partner as a way of compensating for low self-worth, then you'll eventually either devalue them or you'll put them on a pedestal and give them your power. By focusing on their strengths, it confirms and highlights your weaknesses.

Now, if you're trying to find true love, the same principle applies. Your first step is to view the world through the lens of love, to know that love is already with you. Another person can only mirror back to you the degree of self-love you have developed. Whether you are intent upon finding a relationship or deepening the one you're in, it is always important to know that the solution to more or better love is found within yourself. Simply returning to a focus on your inner awareness is, after all, a wonderful starting point for generating self-love. When this has been established as a foundational resource in your Being, then you will never be inclined to turn to another person to fill a void that you feel within your own heart.

It is indeed a provocative and sometimes very challenging question to ask yourself what it means to put your purpose first in the context of your current relationship. Remember, life purpose is not about living in your comfort zone or on autopilot. When it comes to your relationship, there is no gray zone here. It is either a spiritually uplifting and empowering aspect of your life or it is not. Above all, you have to get real with yourself and assess the degree to which your relationship has succumbed to routine or mechanical behavior. If you feel like you know all there is to know about your partner, as if you can no longer see the mysterious or compelling aspects of their nature, then something needs to be shifted in order to return to purpose.

The gray zone that so many marriages succumb to is typified by mediocrity. It is not necessarily bad in the sense of overt fighting or dramatic struggles. Instead, it is just kind of, well, average. Putting your purpose first means that you have no tolerance for this kind of dynamic. You know that your relationship has a sacred purpose and that you deserve so much more than mediocrity.

As you declare this for yourself, you can now see what is preventing you and your partner from experiencing a healthy balance of the sacred purpose of your relationship. Here are a few of the most common obstacles that I've seen in my clinical work:

- Attachment to the belief that love isn't safe
- The need to be right for the sake of control or power. In this sense, one person calls the shots in the relationship and holds all of the power.

- Unresolved trauma that stems from emotional, physical, or sexual abuse
- Attachment to the belief that you're not good enough or complete enough and that you don't deserve true love
- Attachment to past betrayal and heartbreak, which leads to bitterness or disdain for relationships

You get the picture here. These kinds of obstacles can indeed be deeply seeded wounds that profoundly impact our ability to find and keep authentic love. As we bring space to these subconscious holding patterns, we bathe them in a kind of compassionate attention. By putting our purpose first, we are essentially saying that we won't be defined by heartbreak or the need to energetically contract in relation to intimacy. As we see the obstacles that have kept us feeling closed or wounded, we consciously allow in a quality of open-heartedness, tenderness, and deep care for ourselves.

As you awaken the power of your imagination in the context of your relationship, you bring a quality of spontaneity and newness to the relationship. You become more creative in what you offer to your partner, whether it's in what you say to them, the ways you spend your time together, or the gifts you buy them. Awakening your imagination basically means that you're interested in recapturing the spark of the relationship. You don't allow things to go on autopilot.

We are not here to spend time in the gray zone where things are just okay. When you apply the Purpose Principle to your relationship, you will become increasingly clear if there is a true potential for the interchange of spiritual and emotional intimacy or if you are staying in the relationship with the ongoing hope that it will finally become more purposeful. Remember, all you have is now. If the spiritual chemistry isn't there now, will it be there at some undetermined point in the future? Only you can answer that.

CASE STUDY ⚶ DAVID ⚶

By the time he finally made it to my office, David could hardly function. The heartbreak was so severe that he was barely able to breathe. David had found out within the past two weeks that his girlfriend was cheating on him. He literally could not stop thinking about her, as every single second of the day was consumed by obsessive thoughts that centered around the horrible betrayal he felt and the love he still had for her. The pain was so severe that David was wondering if suicide was the only escape.

After probing into David's past with women, it became evident that betrayal had been a recurring theme in his relationships. He had been both the perpetrator and victim on several occasions. This latest situation, however, was far more intense because, as he put it, the love he felt for this woman was unlike anything he had ever known.

David's obstacles to purpose became quite evident within one session of working with him. His entire relationship history was dictated by his subconscious attachment to the belief that love isn't safe. In order to avoid spiritual and emotional intimacy, David would habitually put himself in the role of getting rejected by his partner or of doing the rejecting himself.

With the combination of acupuncture and life coaching, David began to see his current heartbreak in the context of life purpose. It clicked for him that, in order to experience a healthy relationship, he had to develop a higher and deeper level of self-knowledge. He had to become more intimate with himself. By doing this, he would no longer seek love outside of himself and then end up in a situation of betrayal as a means of avoiding intimacy.

Although it required a great deal of commitment, David was able to turn his attention inward and take the focus off of his girlfriend. I encouraged him to think of her as being a mirror for his own mind. Whatever he thought of her was really a projection of what he thought of himself. David brought some space to the drama of calling her and engaging in heated, blame-oriented interactions. While not easy, this was a profound learning experience for David, as the more he brought his awareness inward, the more he could see how he had shunned intimacy his whole life.

Although the process was gradual, David was finally able to experience freedom in the relationship, which was really a by-product of freeing a lifelong belief that love isn't safe. As he healed the deeper wound that brought him into the relationship in the first place, he cut the emotional cord that bound him to his girlfriend. He began a meditation practice as a way to become more spiritually intimate with himself, which gave him faith that he was indeed capable of deep intimacy in a relationship.

THE PURPOSE PRINCIPLE AND HEALTH

Meaning makes a great many things endurable—perhaps everything... Through the creation of meaning... a new cosmos arises. Meaninglessness is... equivalent to illness.

– C a r l   J u n g

In order to understand what it means to bring a sacred purpose to our health, it is very helpful to first define what health actually is. The Western medical definition of health is that it is the absence of disease. You may have already realized that this definition is quite limited and superficial, given that health is defined by what is lacking, in this case disease. The holistic medical definition certainly offers a more vivid definition of health as being a state of vitality or wellness based on the union of body, mind, and spirit.

Having worked with so many patients in a holistic healthcare setting and having coached many holistic practitioners, it has become clear to me that many people get confused about what this actually means. What exactly is the unity of body, mind, and spirit? What does that look like in daily life? If I have migraine headaches, does that mean that my body, mind, and spirit are not integrated? Given that there is a lot of confusion about the concept of health, let's see if we can clarify what health actually is by applying the Purpose Principle.

Here is a new, purpose-based definition of health:

Health is a state of being that occurs when your Spirit is fully expressed through your body and mind.

Remember, the starting point is knowing that we have a sacred purpose.

What is the sacred purpose of our health? To answer this, we must narrow the question down to "What is the sacred purpose of the human body and mind?"

The body/mind complex that each of us is endowed with serves one purpose only: to be a suitable vessel for the expression of our Spiritual nature.

To the extent that our consciousness is clearly and fully expressed through our bodies and minds, we can be said to be dwelling in a state of health. To the extent that we have imbalances or weaknesses in the body/mind complex that block us from the fullest expression of our Spirit, then health is missing.

Think about this new definition for a moment and see if you can identify the staggering implications. From this perspective, health is not defined by our symptoms, cholesterol level, diseases, exercise or dietary habits, blood pressure, or stress level. According to this definition, you could pass your yearly physical with flying colors, exercise five times per week, eat only organic foods—everything on the outside could look really good, and you could still be considered very unhealthy. On the other hand, you could be dying of cancer and still experience a state of health.

Really, how could it be otherwise? One of the main premises of the Purpose Principle is that freedom is available to you now by choosing to activate your Spirit, the nature of your Being that is beyond the small self. This is the foundation of true health. Western medicine, on the other hand, is solely focused on the physiological dimension of health. This model defines health based on the parameters of the body and nervous system. If our sole focus is on the body, however, we will inevitably face a grave disappointment. After all, each and every body will eventually die. No matter how well we care for it, the body is subject to the laws of change and will eventually deteriorate.

It is important to treat the body and mind with respect and care, as doing so will optimize the potential for Spirit to be fully awakened within us. In Traditional Chinese Medicine, it is believed that a number of different elements such as damp, dry, hot, or cold can become imbalanced in the body. These elemental imbalances occur from a variety of factors including:

⊙ Attachment to harmful beliefs and negative emotions

⊙ Poor diet

⊙ Sedentary lifestyle

⊙ Environmental toxins

⊙ Inappropriate use of medications

According to this medical model, you can have too much or too little of any element in your body/mind complex. Any elemental imbalance will greatly increase the likelihood of a spiritual blockage—that is, your consciousness simply cannot be fully alive and awakened within your body/mind due to these elemental obstructions. The intention of acupuncture treatment is to harmonize these elemental imbalances so that you can be more capable of being fully present to your life. Yes, this can also lead to the decrease of various physical or mental symptoms, but that is not really the main objective. Instead, the whole thrust of treatment is to get YOU back, the big YOU that is spiritually based and not identified with the body/mind complex. This is how health is restored according to Traditional Chinese Medicine.

So now we have given health a new definition that clarifies the sacred purpose it has to fulfill in our life. Our degree of health is determined by the extent to which our consciousness is fully accessed and expressed through our bodies and minds. You can now see that you can cultivate a higher degree of health by cultivating a higher state of awareness. By focusing on being before doing, you are realizing that the core influence of health goes deeper than diet, exercise, or stress reduction (these are important factors and there are many resources available to learn more about the best approaches to these lifestyle issues).

Regardless of the relative factors related to your health such as weight, age, blood pressure, or the presence or absence of disease, you can still choose to bring purpose to your health through focusing on and heightening your awareness. This can be such a liberating realization if you have struggled with chronic health concerns or degenerative illness. Keeping this new definition of health in mind, you now know that you can put your purpose first even if your body and mind are in a state of weakness or imbalance. As you do this, you are no longer attached to the need to get rid of your symptoms or discomfort per se. Instead, you perceive each and every sensation and dynamic within your body and mind as containing a sacred lesson that can help you evolve.

Think about how you normally perceive pain, disease, or fatigue. Your normal reaction is likely to try and make it go away. You could do this by utilizing many approaches such as pharmaceutical medications, surgery, or if you're more holistically minded, acupuncture or chiropractic. When you put your purpose first, you are essentially realizing that you are your own best resource for healing. There is nobody and nothing outside of you that can facilitate healing better than you can. Outside intervention (at least holistic approaches) can encourage you to tap into your own wisdom and resources for healing. Ironically, moving toward health doesn't really mean that all of your health problems disappear. Instead, you are able to drop any resistance to what is showing up in your body and mind in this moment, even if it feels painful or frightening. By accepting what is, your Spirit can shine more clearly through your body and mind. This is always the foundation of true healing.

As you move deeper into the process of bringing purpose to your health, you will undoubtedly see what your obstacles are. Every single one of us will say that we want to be healthy, but why do so many of us continue to struggle with both our physical and emotional health? Here are a few of the main obstacles I've witnessed time and again in my acupuncture and life coaching practice:

- Being identified with illness: using sickness or disease as a way to gain attention, sympathy, or validation
- Fear of being accountable to life when you have abundant energy and well-being
- Being reactive instead of proactive: only acknowledging the importance of health when your body is screaming at you in the form of various symptoms
- Making other life themes a higher priority than health: work, money, relationships, etc.

When you bring space to any obstacle to your health, you will understand the connection between body, mind, and spirit. When you see your personal obstacles to health, you will notice that they are actually the root cause of your health problems. You will see that your body is mirroring back to you the quality of your thoughts, emotions, and beliefs all of the time through physical sensation. What you feel in your body is reflective of what is taking place in your mind. If you struggle with chronic pain, then it's likely that you also experience painful thoughts and feelings.[1] You can only realize this when you drop any attachment to your health being other than it is. Who is it that is seeing this relationship between thought and sensation? It is your awareness or Spirit, which is allowed to become fully manifest through the acceptance of what is.

As you become more spacious around these obstacles, you can how create a new version of your health beginning with the awakened power of your imagination. You can use your mind to focus on the sacredness and timelessness of your Being, your Essence that is not at all based in your physical form. You can actually embrace the impermanence of your body and the reality of birth, old age, sickness, and death, which are universal to the human experience. You can free yourself by imagining the nature of your Being that is beyond the body and mind.

Lastly, as you commit to this process day in and day out, your consciousness becomes much more crisp, alert, relaxed, and alive. There is more of a sparkle in your eyes. There is an energetic glow that emanates from your inner Being. Even if your body is still afflicted with chronic or degenerative problems, this sparkle and glow can still arise starting now. When you look at health in this way, it becomes a source of immediate freedom and empowerment.

CASE STUDY)(**JOHN**)(

By the time John first made it to my office, he was desperate for some help. "I feel like there's a knife piercing through the back of my head almost every day and it is getting worse," he confessed with a sigh of pained exhaustion. John's condition had been diagnosed as migraine headaches nearly ten years ago. Over the past few months, the pain had been intensifying to the point that he could barely function. John also reported the following troubling symptoms:

- feeling hot all the time
- high blood pressure
- high cholesterol
- restless sleep
- extreme fatigue
- irritability
- type 2 diabetes

What concerned me most about John's health was the amount of heat and inflammation in his body. Every one of his symptoms pointed to a pattern of severe yin deficiency in Chinese medicine, which means that the cooling, moistening, and calming aspects of his physiology were markedly depleted. In John's case, the extreme degree of heat as it manifested in his specific symptoms suggested that he was highly vulnerable to a heart attack in the not-so-distant future.

When I asked John about his lifestyle, he admitted that he was stuck in a job that he hated. In fact, his job had become so deplorable that he thought every day about how he could possibly find a new direction in his life. But he felt trapped. He was convinced he was too close to retirement to consider leaving his "stable" job in the hope of forging a new path.

I continued to probe into John's life by asking him, "If fear and money weren't obstacles in your life, what would you do?" His answer, which he offered without hesitation, was revealing to say the least.

"I would be a fly fisherman guide. When I'm fishing, it's like all of my troubles fall away. I feel like my old self. Yeah, if I could live on my own terms, that is definitely what I would want to do."

As an acupuncturist steeped in the paradigm of holistic healthcare, this scenario posed a basic quandary: What would it mean to really help John? Sure, his medical doctor had already put him on a host of Western medications to control his blood pressure, diabetes, and cholesterol. John was also taking large doses of Western pain medications to manage the headaches. So it was clear that Western medicine had been trying to help him keep his symptoms at bay so he could feel more comfortable and function better. But was that approach really helping him?

Many alternative health practitioners would do their best to relieve John's concerning symptoms. While there are many skilled healers who could likely help John feel better by offering him herbal or dietary suggestions, or massaging some of the tension out of his body, I wanted to figure out

continued

what it was that John really needed in order to heal. After all, if he was left feeling like he could function better so he could continue on with a job that was not-so-slowly killing him, would that truly offer him the very best care?

One of the strange coincidences of this case is that, right around the time that I first started seeing John, I started reading a book called Healing Beyond the Body by Larry Dossey, M.D. As I was thumbing through this book with John's predicament in the back of my mind, I came across a chapter called "Trout Mind." Intrigued by John's passion for fishing, I read the whole chapter and found it to be a moving account of how fishing is, for many people, a direct gateway to higher states of consciousness.

As I was reveling in the synchronicity of accessing this information right when I started working with John, the realization dawned on me like a thunderbolt: John needed a shift, an awakening in his conscious- ness in order to heal. Focusing exclusively on his physical symptoms will only put a band-aid on the real problem—his true passion in life was being suppressed and it was slowly destroying him.

This suppression was caused by John's attachment to the following beliefs:

- ⊙ Life isn't fair.
- ⊙ You can't do what you really want to do with your life. That is immature or irresponsible.

- You should seek out security even if it means squelching your real passions.
- Get your fair share. There's only so much to go around.
- Life isn't safe.

These were the beliefs that were not only rapidly undermining John's health, but had kept him from a life of peace and balance.

This brings us back to the question of how I could really help John (and the countless people who are experiencing similar blocks in their consciousness). In the time that he's been seeing me, I've been using Chinese medicine to clear all of that heat out of his body, which essentially makes therapeutic suggestions to his psyche that he release these long-held beliefs and seek out the life that he really wants to live. You could say that I am setting an intention in each treatment to help him access his Spirit by dissolving the blocks that prevent it from surfacing.

And I let John borrow the book so he could read the "Trout Mind" chapter. Most of us will only release old beliefs and harmful habits when we feel deeply inspired to do so. I am going to try and fill John with as much inspiration as possible every time I see him. After that, it's up to him to change. Who knows, maybe in a few short months he will be basking in the beauty of the Colorado wilderness fulfilling his dream of being a fly fisherman guide.

If he does, I am willing to bet that his body will thank him in countless ways.

THE EIGHTH STRATEGY

Nothing has a stronger influence psychologically on their environment and especially on their children than the unlived life of the parent.

—Carl Jung

If you are a parent and you have made it this far along the journey of this book, then it's likely that you already understand, at least in theory, the sacredness of your role as a guide, teacher, and caretaker for your children. You have an incredibly vital role to play in the development of your children and—perhaps the perspective that often goes missing—your children also have a sacred contribution to make to your evolutionary process. Let's explore the sacred purpose of parenting from the perspectives of both you and your children.

You could say that the sacred role of the parent is to do whatever it takes to keep the child's Spirit intact, to nurture and develop their core gifts, desires, talents, and passions. These innate attributes become apparent in our children at a very young age. All too often, however, as they mature in their self-image and form more sophisticated beliefs about who they are and why they're here, they lose some of the magic and mystery of their initial spark for life. The parent's sacred role is to help the child not only maintain but to cultivate this spark so it remains an active force in their lives, not something that becomes obscured or buried, which makes the process of maturation that much more difficult.

So, how does the parent do this?

Well, we have to look at the day-to-day mundane interactions we have with our children to determine how much we're helping them keep purpose alive in their consciousness. If we are interested in helping our children live with purpose, the first thing we must do is, you guessed it, look at our own life and assess the degree to which we are applying the Purpose Principle. Are we fully aware and awake to what is happening in this moment? Or are we off somewhere else, lost in fantasy or distracted by our thoughts?

The greatest gift you can offer your children is your full, one-pointed, undistracted, unbridled attention. If you want their Spirit to remain awake, stay committed to expressing your own Spirit. In the context of parenting, this means training yourself to give them 100% of your loving attention as much as possible. Now, this may sound obvious, but think about this concept in your own parenting. How often do you tell your kids to stop doing what they're doing? How often do you subtly push them away and tell them, "Not now, I'm too busy," as if your agenda is more important than theirs? How often do they nag at you and push your buttons and you react with frustration? To summarize, if you really look at your daily interactions with your children, how much of your time do you spend trying to get them to be different than they are?

Now, this is exactly how our children serve a sacred role for us as parents. They are like very powerful teachers that constantly poke at our small self. They are merciless about getting us to drop our personal expectations and agendas. They give us endless opportunities to *surrender*, which is the most profound quality that our children can help to awaken within us. It is up to us, however, to be aware enough in the moment to heed the wisdom of their presence instead of habitually pushing them away.

An important point here is that there are many wonderful, loving, well-intentioned parents who have simply forgotten to be fully awake to what is happening in each moment with their children. Our children starve for this kind of attention from us and often act out in the attempt to get us to fully acknowledge them without distraction. It is very easy to slip into a kind of habitual stance as a parent where you offer your kids a basic level of love and care, but you withhold from them your fullness as a human being. If this strikes a chord with you, please know that this is nothing to feel guilty or negative about.

The good news is that you can choose to change this dynamic right now by putting your sacred purpose as a parent first by allowing in a higher level of awareness with your children. This is the most powerful step you can take to prevent the passing down of your personal obstacles to your kids, let alone the possible traumas that may have been handed down through many familial generations. It is also the only true way to heal the distress and overwhelm you may be feeling as a parent.

What are the main obstacles to parenting with purpose? Well, we just named two of the most common: distress and overwhelm. Many parents are so caught off-guard by the demands of parenting that they literally suffer from a mild form of shock. Many times, this remains a subconscious process. The parent tries to act as if they have it all together, but internally they are struggling with and shocked by how hard parenting actually is, especially if they try to do it perfectly! Really, any of the obstacles to purpose can block us as a parent: fear, negative beliefs or emotions, addictions, or excessive distraction.

Cultivating space around these obstacles, naturally, begins with the realization that they are present. As a parent, you have to be honest with yourself if you are feeling overwhelmed or burdened. Shedding light on what's really happening internally is always the beginning step to freedom. Then, you can always use your children as a reference point for cultivating more space. You can do this by giving them more space to be who they are. Allow them to show up with all of their imperfection, quirkiness, and annoying habits. Give them space to express their unbounded youthfulness. As you do this, you are giving yourself space as well. You are letting go of the need to do parenting "right" or to be in control.

Let's be clear here that this does not mean that you just let your kids do whatever they please. The idea is that, as you heighten your awareness and drop your resistance to your children, you are now able to set healthy boundaries and impose a balanced level of discipline upon them. Not too tight, not too loose. You always have their needs in your conscious awareness, but you don't cross the line of habitually trying to control or change them.

Your children also serve a sacred role for you by showing you how to live with awakened imagination. Children often exhibit a spontaneous and whimsical quality of playfulness that is intimately connected to their imagination. They help us to see that life purpose is replete with this kind of playfulness and spontaneity. When we take things too seriously, we have usually strayed from our purpose. If you have been wondering how to use your imagination in the way we have described in this book, simply start observing children. Make it a point to watch how they play, and how energetically light they are as they carry themselves in space.

The last strategy that creates the foundation of the Purpose Principle, commitment, is perhaps the aspect of this process that sounds very serious. And, yes, there is a seriousness about staying committed to your purpose in all realms of life. After all, that is what you are here to do. But with that seriousness and intensity, there is always a quality of lightheartedness and playfulness. Allow your parenting to become an expression of this union between intensity and playfulness. You have an intensity for being awake to this moment and, once you are, you step into the reality of youthful whimsicality and joy that children so magically convey.

Utilize Purpose in Every Moment

3 Practical Steps to Make the Purpose Principle a Part of Your Daily Life

If you are waiting for anything to live and love without holding back, then you suffer. Every moment is the most important moment of your life. No future time is better than now to let down your guard and love.

— David Deida

All of the strategies you have learned have given you a new way of relating to your life. In this strategy, let's discuss specific things you can do on a daily basis to enhance your commitment to what you have learned up to this point. It is important that we anchor these strategies into your daily experience so that they actually penetrate your life instead of remaining abstract concepts. Some of these practical steps have to do with clearing out external obstacles that can impede your evolution, while others focus more on how to actually practice these strategies all of the time. After all, that is the goal: to be in a constant dialogue with ourselves about our purpose and to be receptive to what is showing up in our reality so that we can keep moving forward. The steps you will learn in this lesson are powerful methods for developing your ability to do this so that the fabric of your daily life begins to change for the better.

Step 1: Practice purposeful awareness — how to meditate, pray, and have mindful interactions with humanity

You have already heard several times by now that it's helpful to think of the Purpose Principle as a practice that requires continual refinement. It is a practice to be fully present to life so you know who you are and what you have to offer. You may have wondered how you can actually practice being present to your life aside from simply choosing to do so.

MEDITATION — AN ANCIENT TECHNIQUE
TO EXPERIENCE SPACE

Meditation is the practice of freedom. It has been used by numerous cultures over thousands of years as a way out of suffering. In essence, meditation is really a concentrated and direct practice of the fifth strategy: focusing on the space that surrounds your reality. Meditation is all about the cultivation of space, which is the primary entry point of freedom. Without space, we suffer. With space, we can breathe. We can see life from a more elevated perspective.

In the Western world, meditation has largely been associated with various health benefits, from lowering blood pressure, anxiety, and stress, to helping with insomnia, depression, and fatigue. While all of this can indeed result from regular practice, these healing benefits are really just by-products of a much deeper phenomenon: the cultivation of space. In many Eastern spiritual traditions, recognizing space as one's own nature is synonymous with enlightenment, which, in the context we are discussing here, can be defined as the complete expression of and unification with our life purpose.

While all of this may sound far-removed from your current life experience, it is vital to know that you have direct access in this very moment to this enlightened state, this purposeful place within you that is untouched by all of the conditions of daily life. Meditation is perhaps the most direct and powerful practice we have as human beings to access this state of spaciousness.

When I first started meditating , I was completely baffled as to what the whole point of it was. I found myself sitting in an uncomfortable position, watching my mind, observing the moment-to-moment content of my thoughts and feelings. The whole process was honestly torturous. Everything I had read suggested that meditation was supposed to induce an exalted, peaceful, and liberated state of being that would take me away from my mundane agonies and tribulations. But that was certainly not my experience as a beginning practitioner. I felt just the opposite. I struggled to make it through even 20 minutes on the meditation cushion. As I watched the content of my thoughts, I became quite convinced that I was completely nuts. It was not only astonishing, but appalling to realize the massive speed and contradiction that was playing out in my thoughts on a moment-to-moment basis.

I came very close to giving up entirely on this practice. I honestly felt like it was making my life worse, like my insane thoughts were becoming even more amplified through regular practice. What I have realized after teaching so many people how to meditate is that this is a very common, if not typical, experience for beginning meditators. You see, all that meditation is doing in the initial phases is getting you to see what's actually taking place in your mind on a moment-to-moment basis. It's not like the practice is making your thoughts worse or more visceral. Those thoughts are there all the time, which is the truly scary part! Meditation is just getting you to see the actual content of your inner being.

The first step of this practice is just that: Seeing what's actually happening inside of you. This is the beginning of creating space. What you are creating space from is the continual stream of thought and feeling that you normally identify as you. When your personal identity is wrapped around this continual stream of mental and emotional activity, there is absolutely no space to consider a larger perspective on your situation as a human being. You see, purpose arises when you can see the space around the small self that is bound up in habitual thought and feeling.

Now, as you learn to meditate, the most crucial part of the practice is that you go into it without any attachment whatsoever. You simply do the practice for the sake of doing it. You are not expecting to be less stressed, more calm, a better person, or more evolved. You are doing it as a basic expression of self-care. This is the part that trips people up: The evolutionary, healing, liberating benefits of meditation can only surface when you drop the need to be evolved, healed, or liberated. You are not looking for anything out of the practice. You are not trying to calm your mind, shut down your thoughts, or be more peaceful. You are simply present to what is. That's it.

Whether the content of your mind is painful or pleasurable, you simply notice what is happening without judgment or resistance. You don't try to make it more positive or healthy. You simply rest your attention in pure awareness. In this sense, there is infinite room for anything that shows up in your field of consciousness. This infinite room is space, and space is what heals. Space is infinity. It has no boundaries, no limitations. It is, in essence, who you are. Your capacity for genius, your innate talents, your passion, creativity, and aspirations—all of this arises out of space.

Meditation is a means of harnessing your personal capacity for wisdom and truth. It is a gateway to this sacred realm of existence that can only be accessed by dropping your conventional identity and plunging into the mysterious depths of your true nature. As you begin a meditation practice, you will likely bump up against the frenzied nature of your own mind. You will vividly see any tendency you have toward inner conflict, depression, negative beliefs—really the entire gamut of obstacles and subconscious holding patterns described in the fourth strategy—become apparent when you meditate on a daily basis. If this is your experience, please keep this in mind:

> *Simply being willing to see and create space around the content of your own mind, no matter how frenzied, conflicted, judgmental, or stressful it appears, is a tremendous act of kindness toward yourself. This in itself is a sacred act.*

The following is a basic meditation exercise that will help you truly integrate all that you have learned up to this point. The practice of meditation really is a microcosm for all of these strategies: it gets you anchored in present moment reality; it certainly helps you focus on being before doing; it enables you to clearly see your obstacles; it brings about the recognition of space around those obstacles; it can be a powerful way to enhance your faculty of imagination; and it is definitely a practice that develops our ability to commit to what is most essential.

> *Find a comfortable place to sit, either upright in a chair or cross-legged on a meditation cushion. Close your eyes. Make sure your spine is straight but without strain. Take a moment to relax your shoulders, stomach, chest, throat, and face. Allow your chest to open, as if you are*

assuming a stance of dignity in relation to whatever arises during the meditation. Your posture is both relaxed and alert. You are at rest but fully present.

Now, take several deep slow breaths through your nose, filling your belly deeply and exhaling slowly. Let go of any tension or distress in your body. Once you have settled into this, resume normal breathing. Set an intention for your practice. You could say silently to yourself, "I intend to use this time to uncover my purpose," or "I intend to use this time to awaken to who I really am and the reason I am here."

Allow this intention to reverberate through your being so it has a ripple effect on the duration of your practice. Now, bring your awareness to a place of one-pointed stillness within you. Rest your full faculty of attention in this place of pure silence. This does not mean that you try to force yourself to stop thinking. Let your thoughts and feelings come and go, making sure that you don't attach to them and take their content personally.

Just let them arise and pass away, simply keeping your focus on this place of pure stillness within you. Rest your mind in this stillness for several moments, allowing yourself to sink deeper into this process with each inhale and exhale. See if you can identify with the silence that underlies your thoughts. Even if your mind is racing with things that have to be done, reflections on what has already happened, or any other kind of fantasy, simply notice this and stay focused on the underlying silence. No resistance, no fighting with yourself. Just letting be whatever arises, then with just as much ease, letting it pass away.

See if you can keep your focus on the space around your thoughts and feelings, regardless of what is transpiring in your mind. Whether painful or pleasurable, do not resist or crave what you notice unfolding in your mind.

You may notice that your thoughts cease entirely, if only for a moment. Allow yourself to rest in the gap between your thoughts. If this does not happen, no need to judge yourself. Just continue with the practice. After several minutes, it is normal if your concentration starts to wane somewhat. If this happens, see if you can reverse this so that each inhale brings you that much deeper into stillness, each exhale letting go of anything inside that does not serve you.

Remember, you are not trying to stop your thoughts. It is more a matter of using your awareness to stay at rest, dwelling in inner stillness, even if you are thinking. This may feel awkward at first, which is totally normal.

Now, take several deep, slow breaths again. Set an intention as you close your practice to extend whatever freedom or peace you have found within yourself out to the world. Feel free to make some slight movements. Roll your shoulders and your neck several times. Open your eyes when you are ready.

By committing to a practice as simple as this for even a few minutes a day, your entire life can change very quickly. It is like hitting the fast-forward button on your personal evolution. That is why people have meditated across the planet for thousands of years. (Remember, everyone's experience is unique. The practice itself is an act of self-love, even if it feels like it's taking you down the opposite road of personal evolution.)

Many people find that their meditation practice is what keeps them consistently grounded in their purpose. They simply could not stay present to their life without a daily practice and reminder of who they are and why they are here. Indeed, there are so many forces in our world that can distract us from the core reason we are here that it may be essential to commit to a practice such as this on a daily basis. Many people find that even as little as 15 minutes a day can be profoundly helpful in staying anchored to purpose.[1]

PRAYER—OPENING UP TO THE GREAT MYSTERY

Whether you believe in the conventional notion of God or not, you can still experience profound benefit from daily prayer. Even if you are an atheist or have historically regarded religion with suspicion or cynicism, you can likely acknowledge that there is an incredibly mysterious force to this universe that lies outside of the boundaries of your intellectual understanding. Put simply, 15 billion years ago, something came out of nothing. How in the world did that happen? There is something deeply compelling about the simple contemplation of this question. You could look at prayer as the daily ritual of contemplating the mystery of life itself. Prayer allows you to put your awareness into the largest context possible, to view yourself and your purpose through the lens of this ultimate mystery. Holding your mind in this awareness can be an awe-inspiring and humbling process. Prayer is ultimately the practice of surrendering our personal control to the will of the universe. It is a way of paying reverence to the infinite forces that move through and beyond us.

Many of us have been taught to pray to a force outside of ourselves that is much more powerful than we are. Especially during times of hardship, we turn to this external protector for guidance and help. The strategies you have learned up to this point, however, embrace a perspective that encourages you to see that power as dwelling inside of you as much as it does outside of you. In this way, you can actually pray to the highest—or deepest—part of yourself, which is inseparable from the universe as a whole. When you have this understanding of your inner power, you would feel compelled to pray all of the time because it is a way of staying in contact with your true nature. Even when things are going really well, you have a daily ritual of prayer that keeps you attuned to your higher purpose. Instead of just asking for help from God or the universe, prayer is a time of expressing gratitude and deepening the reflection on how you can unleash your deepest capacity to help. It is a time to say thank you for who you are and what you have.

The most powerful moments of prayer that I've had are when I'm not really asking for anything in particular. I'm really just acknowledging what I already have and thanking the Divine for that. I've had to train my mind to focus on what's already working in my life and express gratitude for that rather than offer up the desires I have based on what's lacking. This really is a training process because our modern world focuses so much on what is missing. It has become increasingly apparent to me that we will only get more of something when we focus on what we already have and stop perceiving present moment reality as a problem. In this sense, prayer is like a ritual of offering gratitude for what is already here. It is an acknowledgment of the inherent completion and perfection of this moment.

MEDITATION AND PRAYER IN EVERY MOMENT

The whole point of meditation and prayer is that they make an impact on your daily life. Can you meditate while you wash the dishes, drive your kids to school, or talk with a friend on the phone? Remember our first definition of life purpose: an awareness of present moment reality. The primary reason you are here is to be fully here! You are here to be fully awake to this moment. Out of this, all of your personal greatness can come alive.

If you really pay attention, however, you'll likely notice that there are many times during each and every day where your attention drifts away from the present moment. Jon Kabat-Zinn, a wonderful meditation teacher, wrote a book called *Wherever You Go, There You Are*. This title perfectly captures the intention of meditation as it relates to life purpose. In whatever moment you find yourself, are you fully here, free, unobstructed, uncluttered, pure, and one-pointed in your awareness? Every single moment you are alive gives you the opportunity to access your purpose in this way.

See if you can bring a quality of meditation to every aspect of your life experience. Can your words be infused with awareness and spaciousness? Can you train yourself to bring purpose to each and every word that you speak? Everything you say makes a profound impact on the world. How would your life change if you brought a quality of clear awareness and intention to every word you utter? Can you listen with purpose? What would that look like? When you bring your full capacity of awareness to someone else, you are offering them something precious. Can you see that person from their own side? Truly identify with the lens they see the world through? There is a freedom in doing so.

The Purpose Principle applies to every moment—good or bad, happy or sad. When you bring purpose to your daily life through meditation and prayer, your worldview begins to expand and you have so much more to offer yourself and others.

Step 2: Purposefully monitor what you allow into your life

When you focus on being before doing, you see that your outer world is always a mirror for your inner world. This means that everything that shows up in your outer circumstances is mirroring back your state of mind. In this step, it's time to take an inventory of the stuff in your outer life and see if it matches up with the purpose-based shifts you've made in your inner life.

THE PURPOSE OF OTHER PEOPLE— ESTABLISHING A SACRED SUPPORT SYSTEM

Let's start by looking at the people that you surround yourself with on a daily basis. You can make a list of the people you interact with most consistently, whether in your job, social circles, or other environments. Now, spend some time contemplating each of these relationships and determine for yourself if the quality of interaction you generally engage in with each person is uplifting, empowering, and inspiring. When you commit to purpose above all else, you want all of your interactions to reflect these qualities. The people that are closest to you are holding up a very clear mirror for how you feel about yourself. When you stop to examine your relationships in this way, you may find that you use certain people to enable your own frustration or pain. Other people can serve as a powerful distraction from your own inner emptiness.

As a way of avoiding the bigger picture of our purpose, we can use other people as a form of entertainment, by forging alliances that are based on gossiping about coworkers or friends, or by engaging in conversation that has no real substance to it. In this common dynamic, our relationships serve as an outer block to purpose. We are using people to stay stuck in a painful or unfulfilling reality.

As with everything we have discussed up to this point, we have a choice when it comes to who we allow into our lives and how each relationship unfolds. Even if we are stuck in the same physical environment as a coworker who rubs us the wrong way or we have a dysfunctional family member whose presence we can't escape from, we can still choose to be purposeful in our interactions. We can cultivate a truthful relationship with ourselves and extend that out to every relationship we have with others. When we bring this kind of intention to our inner reality, we have no tolerance for interpersonal dynamics that promote negativity, judgment, or distraction. We will either choose to remove certain people from our lives, or if we aren't able to do so, we will do our very best to remain internally aware in their presence. We won't allow them to steal our power or bring us down to their level.

The relationships you choose will either be a strong catalyst for or obstacle to the unfolding of your purpose. As you put your purpose first and commit to it above all else, choose relationships that will serve as a sacred support system to help you evolve. Surround yourself with people who have the same level of commitment.

THE VIRTUE OF SIMPLICITY—
ELIMINATE THE UNNECESSARY

As you take inventory of the relationships in your life, another very helpful step is to take inventory of the stuff in your life. Now, let's be clear right off the bat that you can have freedom in your life whether you have a ton of material goods or very few. What you have isn't the point. Instead, we want to take a look at the metaphor behind your material possessions.

What purpose does your stuff serve in your life? Do you own a variety of things that don't have a sacred purpose? You just kind of ended up taking these things along for the ride? The material goods that lack purpose in your life are the things you want to clear out, just like you'd want to clear out negative or draining relationships that don't really serve you. The operative word here is clutter. Just as with the people you allow into your life, the stuff you accumulate is a mirror for your own mind. To the extent that you have a lot of material things that lack a real purpose in your life, you can safely assume that your mind is cluttered with the baggage of unhelpful beliefs and emotions.

Now, how do you determine if the stuff you have has a real purpose in your life? One simple way to clarify this is to determine if the things you own have a direct and relevant value to you now; if you're holding on to them because they had some meaning or purpose in the past; or if you feel that they may in the future. If they're not helpful and relevant to your life now, then it would likely be helpful to clear them out of your life.

It takes a certain amount of courage and self-knowledge to buck the modern Western trend of material accumulation. Many people find that, once they do, they uncover a freedom and joy that had been buried (literally and metaphorically) by all the stuff they had acquired. Simplicity is closely aligned with purpose. This does not mean that you have to live like Thoreau and spend your life in the woods. What it does mean is that you live your life consciously, on your terms. Everything you allow into your life, you do it purposefully and mindfully, knowing that it too is impermanent. You can't take it with you when you die. When you keep this in mind, you may have a higher standard for what you allow into your life!

THE MEDIA, MARKETING,
AND INFORMATION OVERLOAD

Every single day, the average person is exposed to 3,000 advertisements. When you think about what advertisements actually are, an attempt to persuade you to stop what you're doing to consider how a product will make your life better, often by getting you to feel that you're not enough right now, then it is clear why we need to bring a sense of purpose to the mass media and information overload that we are all exposed to.

One extreme is to throw away your TV, stop reading the newspaper, and try your best to avoid exposure to the onslaught of marketing messages and information that surround you. The other end of the spectrum is willingly giving several hours of your life every day to watch TV, read the newspaper, or surf the Internet. Perhaps the most purposeful place to begin is to focus on being before doing. This would entail keeping your eyes wide open as you are exposed to the mass media. What happens to the quality of your awareness as you watch TV or read the paper? Do you feel fully alive, energized, and excited? Or do you feel like your senses have been blanketed? When you watch the nightly news, do you feel that much closer to your purpose? Or do you feel further away from it, as if you've received confirmation that the world is really screwed up and there's not much you can do about it?

If you can pay attention in this way, you will never be enslaved by the mass media, for its power is 100% dependent upon our lack of awareness.

Now, when you keep your eyes open, it is likely that, sooner or later, you'll have very little interest in spending your time watching other people on TV or reading about the atrocities of the world in the daily paper. As your awareness increases, so will your desire for activities that promote harmony, joy, and connection. Imagine for a moment how your life would look if it were completely and totally free of clutter. No negative people. No possessions that weigh you down. No mindless exposure to the mass media, marketing propaganda, and information overload. As you purposefully monitor what you allow into your life, you can finally breathe deeply. You can live life on your terms based on your awakened imagination. Your outer life can serve as a perfect mirror for your inner life, which is aligned with your greater purpose.

Step 3: Consciously choose how you give of yourself—how you give is more important than how much you give

While it is true that life purpose always comes back to giving of yourself for the benefit of others, it is important to keep in mind that even giving can be an obstacle to purpose. Whether it's your time, money, or energy, giving isn't really what matters. Instead, it is the intention or motivation behind what you give that determines how closely aligned with purpose it is. Giving can come from a place of pure generosity or it can be a form of validation for the small self.

Generosity can only underlie your giving when you know your purpose-based Self. That is, you know your limitations, needs, and boundaries in relation to what you have to offer. In this way, you need not operate out of a place of "should," guilt, or societal expectation. You don't overextend yourself nor do you withhold the positive offerings you have to make.

When giving is stemming from the small self, it can be yet another form of distraction that prevents us from truly seeing our greater purpose. Our mainstream values promote the need to stay busy, with a constant to-do list. Because of this, it is easy to become lost in a whirlwind life where we lose ourselves to the endless responsibilities we have taken on. Part of us feels validated and useful for staying so busy, while another part of us is craving for rest and feels exhausted. I have had countless numbers of patients who came to see me after discovering, much to their confusion, that their bodies were shutting down with fatigue, anxiety, insomnia, PMS, and a host of other chronic symptoms. They simply couldn't figure out why they were struggling with their health. After all, they were doing the all of the "right" things — staying busy, running their kids around, throwing parties, getting involved in the PTA meetings, making meals, going to the gym, and taking care of all the myriad details of daily life. They were basically giving their time and energy away all day, every day.

While there is nothing wrong with doing these activities, it is all about how we relate to them and what our purpose is in initiating them. Why do we choose (and yes, it is a choice) to take on so much? Look at your situation. What would happen if you made the choice to completely cut out any activities or routines that weren't absolutely necessary? When you stop habitually giving your time and energy away, you are put face to face with space. Your life slows down and you start to see the subtleties of your own nature. You get a glimpse of the big question mark of the ultimate purpose of doing so much all of the time. You see space.

Recognizing space is always at the core of truly generous giving. When you are tapped into the space of your nature, there is no "I" that seeks validation through staying excessively busy. You have no need for distraction or speed. When this is the case, what you give becomes immensely more powerful. You see that sometimes you must give to yourself by slowing down and putting your needs first. As long as it's coming from this place of awareness and spaciousness, this commitment to self-care can be a profound act of generosity. Self-reflection is a basic human need that is the only true antidote to the collective overwhelm and exhaustion so many of us feel in the modern age.

If you are the type to fill your plate with too much, make it a practice to lean into the space that surrounds your busyness. Give yourself permission to slow down and create healthy boundaries around the demands that others place on you and that you place on yourself. Remember that awareness of the present moment and the identification of your innate gifts, aspirations, and potential come from a place of receptivity. Your primary and most sacred role is to be receptive to your purpose in this way, which is an incredible act of generosity.

The more you practice living with purpose, the more you actually become your purpose. You become increasingly unified with the sacred role you have to play. The deeper your experience of this unity becomes, the less tolerance you have for anything that distracts you from living in present moment reality and expressing your innate gifts to the world.

Section III is about the fruition of life purpose. It will give you a powerful glimpse into how life looks when you become your purpose and fully embrace the totality and impermanence of each and every moment.

Section 3

THE FRUITION
of the
Purpose Principle

Become Your Purpose
The 4 Attributes of the
Purposeful Person

*We have what we seek, it is there all the time, and
if we give it time, it will make itself known to us.*

—Thomas Merton

Believe it or not, it's highly likely that you've already had many direct experiences of your life purpose coming to fruition. You've had moments of being fully plugged into your deeper nature as a human being, fully alive to this moment, expressing the very best that is within you. The only problem is that your direct experience of the Purpose Principle has likely been sporadic. You have had the occasional flash of infinite space that surrounds the small self, but your day-to-day life is still about trying to wade through both the inner and outer obstacles to purpose.

The fruition of life purpose doesn't have to be some sort of grandiose event that shakes the entire cosmos. It can be as simple as having your senses fully awakened to the beauty and mystery of the clouds that hover overhead. If you've had the experience of losing yourself in a creative endeavor, conversation, athletic event, or providing a service for someone, as if time doesn't exist and hours feel like minutes, then you have had a taste of your purpose. In a sense, these moments are liberating and therapeutic and, in another sense, they can be quite ordinary.

The point is to awaken your innate ability to live with purpose all of the time.

Given that you have very likely experienced sporadic contact with your greater purpose, then it is indeed possible to nourish the development of purposeful experience so it eventually becomes the way you live on a consistent basis.

What we are getting at here is that it's crucial that you don't look at the information in this strategy as being a far-removed ideal from the life that you currently have. You have already tasted what we are talking about here. It's simply a matter of deepening your relationship with the Purpose Principle so that it is always at the forefront of your awareness, intentions, and actions.

Everything we are discussing in this strategy is accessible to you in this moment. You have all of the inner resources you need to bring your purpose to fruition. Consider the sacred purpose of your own life as it currently stands. This is always the first step toward the Purpose Principle coming to full fruition in your life.

When we talk about the fruition of the Purpose Principle, it's important to remember that living with purpose is a dynamic, ever-changing process that requires ongoing commitment. No matter how evolved you are, it always boils down to a choice in each moment to be fully here now without attachment to your obstacles or a habitual resistance to what is. It takes courage to be clear about what you really want aside from your own or other peoples' expectations or judgments. And it requires an ongoing willingness to be truthful with yourself in order to implement those aspirations into reality and consistently bring your spiritual vision into the physical world. While there is never a point where the Purpose Principle becomes static, it's also helpful to remember that there is always a quality of effortlessness and fluidity to the fruition of life purpose. Keep in mind the paradox that it is the hardest thing you'll ever do and it is completely effortless at the same time.

It is also helpful to keep in mind that you don't become infallible when your life purpose comes to fruition. You will still make mistakes. You'll still get bumped off course on occasion. You can still have various hardships, illnesses, or setbacks. The defining difference is that your *relationship* with anything that happens has now gone through a radical transformation. As you'll see by looking at the following four attributes, the lens you see the world through is now steeped in freedom and generosity, regardless of the circumstances that are presented to you.

Let's take a look at the four attributes of the purposeful person, all the while keeping in mind that each of these attributes is within you already.

THE FOUR ATTRIBUTES OF THE
PURPOSEFUL PERSON

1 You have space around your thoughts, obstacles, and limitations and, as a result, you can clearly identify your gifts, aspirations, and potential.

When you become your purpose, you are no longer bound up in attachment to what you think. If you pay close attention, you'll notice that your thoughts quite often serve as a means of keeping the obstacles to purpose intact. Even if it feels subtle, see if you notice that your day-to-day thoughts carry a general undercurrent of stress, fear, guilt, blame, judgment, speed, doubt, or confusion. Attachment to what we think is a primary form of nourishment for the small self. When our thinking is unconscious, meaning that we're not really aware of the momentary stream of mental activity taking place in our minds, then thought can very much dictate what kind of meaning we form in reaction to our life experience.

Our unconscious thoughts carry the energetic undercurrent of our obstacles. Our lack of awareness perpetuates and amplifies these obstacles. A purposeful person is one who is generally aware of the content of their mind. They don't allow their thoughts to sabotage their heartfelt objectives or desires. They have space around their mental activity.

In my experience, having space around thought is much more helpful than trying to manufacture positive thoughts. In this sense, I prefer the term purposeful thinking rather than positive thinking. That is, when we think, we think with awareness. If we are experiencing a lot of pain in our thoughts, we allow that pain to be present without resisting it.

As we do this, we see the space around our thoughts. We know that thought is not real. It is merely a form of energy that is playing out in our field of awareness. It is an illusion. When we live with purpose, there is always a basic level of knowing the illusory nature of our thoughts. Whether they seem to be good or bad, we don't get attached to them. This understanding of thought is essentially what leads us to the awakening of our imagination. When we are not ruled by habitual thinking, we can proactively and purposefully guide the content that takes place in our minds. We are moving out of the linear, conditioned, and habitual mode of thought that only feeds our obstacles. We are using our awareness to open the doorway to a place of inner power and wisdom that clearly shows us who we really are and the best that we have to offer this world. As a result of this wisdom, we move closer to the life that we really want, the one is that is aligned with our deeper nature.

Seeing the space around your thoughts is a direct and immediate way to realize how unstoppable you are when you choose to live with purpose. As long as you are not attached to the extremes of doubt and fear that ride the wavelength of unconscious thought, there is absolutely no one and nothing that can hold you back. This is what it means to "get out of your own way." In my own experience, life has taken on a completely new form now that I am no longer solely identified with unconscious thought. My productivity level has skyrocketed, my use of time has become much more efficient and one-pointed, and my desire to offer the best of myself continues to accelerate and expand.

And yes, it is also true that when you access and express your gifts, aspirations, and potential, you will experience bursts of spiritual joy and satisfaction in your life that you never dreamed possible. You, too, have access to this purpose-based joy. It is within you right now, but it can only arise through nonattachment.

2 **You surrender to what life brings to you at any given time. You put yourself in the right situations because you know yourself.**

You've probably heard that living with purpose is all about serving others and giving your life away. While it is true that your entire life becomes a vehicle for helping others, what's most important is that your inner reality is based on true generosity and freedom. What this means is that you know how and when to give of yourself. You don't give just because you feel like you should or to ease a guilty conscience.

Many people try to base their life on service, but deep down they are swallowing resentment or feel burned out from the role that they play in life. Think of all the jobs and roles out there that have a truly altruistic nature to them: nurses, counselors, caretakers, stay-at-home moms, people who care for their elderly parents, waiters, and so on. All of these roles exemplify giving your time away to serve others, but how many people are really thriving in these roles? How many are truly tapped into their sacred purpose as they wait on or care for others?

It takes a high level of emotional and spiritual maturity to give in a way that is truly uplifting and empowering. When you have actualized the Purpose Principle, it is clear that giving and receiving are part of the same energetic process. You experience the deepest form of spiritual nourishment when you give fully of yourself. If you are feeling resentful, exhausted, or overwhelmed, however, then your motivation for giving is based in the small self. You have to use the signals coming from your body, mind, and environment to know if you are giving in an authentic way.

Many of us focus on the outer form of generosity, such as donating money to charities or spending time at the local soup kitchen. While such activities can indeed be very purposeful ways to be of service, it is always important to remember that the ultimate source of giving is being clear and present in your own consciousness. It always comes back to being before doing. In this sense, you can energetically offer a compassionate intention to someone walking down the street. You can spend some time imagining someone you know who is suffering overcoming their obstacles. You can energetically send that person a wish for liberation through the power of your own mind.

Generosity begins as a state of mind and extends out to our actions. Before rushing out to commit all kinds of purposeful activities, become intimate with the felt sense of generosity in your own mind and heart. Get to know how it feels to be truly generous to yourself and others. If you put your focus here first, then your actions will naturally become more generous. There will be an integrity that enables others to trust you. In this context, integrity means that what you say and what you do match up with how you really feel. Your inner and outer realities are congruent.

Other people will only begin to fully confide in and trust you when you know yourself in this way, when you become intimately familiar with the energy of generosity in your own being. In the moment that you're dwelling in a generous state of being, there are no gaps or black holes in your character. You have shed light on all of your obstacles, and you are no longer bound by the unconscious stream of thoughts giving you an endless barrage of conflicting input. You are aligned. Is this subject to change? Sure it is. Every moment is new. That is why commitment is so important, which in this context means returning to the energy of generosity over and over regardless of what your external circumstances bring to you.

When this happens, other people begin to turn to you as a resource, a solace, a kind of inspiring and honest presence that they can fall back on. The kind of generosity that arises when you apply the Purpose Principle is enormously compelling and helpful to other people. It not only inspires them, it is the single most powerful thing you can do to help them be free, to encourage them to wake up. You may have even noticed that for you to be as far along as you are on the path to purpose, there have been maybe a couple pivotal figures whose presence alone have mysteriously guided you to move beyond the small self. Now it's your turn to set that same example for others. If you choose to, you can become a role model to countless others starting right now.

3 Inspiration And Creative Joy: The Hallmarks Of Purposeful Living

Expressing our purpose to the world is by far the most inspiring process we could ever undertake. It inspires other people more than anything else. There is nothing more helpful to people than when they see someone living with purpose. When you are demonstrating purpose through inspired action, you are helping others to embark on the same path. You are helping them break free of their own bondage. That is how powerful inspiration can be.

More than anything else, each of us wants to be inspired. We want to feel a force that can instantly pull us out of our limitations and struggles. We want to know the freedom and power that come from being plugged into our infinite potential.

When you commit to your purpose, your very presence helps others brush up against their own purpose. Sometimes, if they are steeped in resistance or attached to their obstacles, this can freak people out or make them angry, and they will have a hard time being around you. They will only taste this inspired energy when they are ready for it. Knowing that you are capable of inspiring others keeps your commitment to your purpose strong, even if it means being judged or pushed away by people who are identified with the small self. You feed off the strength and energy that inspiration brings you, which enables you to keep moving forward.

One of the hallmarks of inspiration is the wonderful feeling of effortless creativity that it produces. When we are inspired, we truly are accessing a higher—or deeper—place within ourselves that knows nothing about force or fear. This place is fully unified with the limitless creative energy of the universe. When we are inspired, we are in no way blocked from this magical source of creativity. Because of this, inspired ideas arise in our minds out of nowhere. We get flashes of genius that feel as natural as can be. We have "Aha!" moments where we say to ourselves, "This is so obvious! Why didn't I think of this before?"

Indeed, the flashes of brilliance that enter into our consciousness feel as obvious and normal as anything else that we perceive in material reality. Inspiration is the key that unlocks these states of mind. It is an invitation to a greater presence within ourselves that feeds off the amazing power of this universe. Inspiration invokes this genius into us. We serve as a vessel for its expression. It cannot be forced or contrived by our small self. It moves through us, seizing us for brief moments when we completely lose ourselves in whatever inspires us. Just imagine what your life would be like if these brief moments became your ordinary day-to-day experience! When we live with purpose, this is not only possible, but to be expected.

Living in a state of creative joy does not necessarily mean that you feel happy all of the time. Instead, think of it in this way: The backdrop of your experience as a human being is based on being energized and excited by what you do each and every day. When you are expressing your innate gifts, aspirations, and potential each day that you live, then you will wake up in the morning with a sense of excitement for what the day will bring. Yes, you will still feel occasional bouts of pain, fear, or disappointment, but the general tone of your life is steeped in the highly uplifting qualities of inspiration and creative joy. As long as you are human, the obstacles to purpose will make their presence known. As you bring space to them, however, they become more transparent, less overwhelming, and ultimately they arise with much less force and frequency. The creative joy of expressing your purpose arises directly out of the space you have cultivated around your obstacles. It arises naturally, as it is the deepest expression of your innate nature surfacing.

There is a danger in romanticizing these qualities of inspiration and creative joy because it's likely you will feel as if these states are separate from you in this moment. You can still be who you are, right now, with all of the challenges you face and tap into your inner capacity for inspiration and creative joy. Yes, these qualities can be wonderful, magical, and even blissful—but you need not become attached to these either.

Just as the obstacles are within you, so is the space around those obstacles and the purposeful qualities that arise out of that space. If you get attached to these more purposeful qualities by trying to solidify around them and identify with them as who you are, they will quickly lose their real magic. In this way, even purposeful qualities can become obstacles if we attach to them. All of the "good stuff" arises out of space and dissolves back into space. It is all impermanent. If you hold this truth within yourself, then you can immerse yourself in the creative joy of your life without latching on to it as a permanent or solid thing.

4 You realize the preciousness of who you are, of being human, and of life itself

A purposeful person not only believes in the preciousness of life, they actually *experience* life as a precious event. They live and breathe this quality of preciousness, which is reflected in the quality of their intentions and actions. In particular, a purposeful person is one who has experienced the preciousness of being human, of who they uniquely are, and of life itself. Let's look at each of these in some depth.

1 **The preciousness of being human.** As a human being, you have the perfect blend of qualities necessary to live with purpose. Unlike other forms of life, you are intelligent and self-aware enough to know that you have a sacred purpose to fulfill in your life. You also have likely experienced just enough suffering to encourage the questioning of who you are and why you are here. Many ancient wisdom traditions assert that it is a precious and rare opportunity to be born as a human being. The potential for purpose-based evolution is immediately accessible as long as the person has enough awareness of and interest in their innate ability to utilize this opportunity.

As there are 7 billion other human beings inhabiting planet Earth at this time, it may be hard to see why being born as a human is such a rare and precious opportunity. When you tap into the space beyond the small self, however, you begin to sense how vast the universe actually is. Even on planet Earth, there are so many billions of life forms that simply don't have the capacity for self-awareness.

According to many of the ancient wisdom traditions, there are countless forms of life that we humans cannot perceive with our senses that either live in alternate dimensions of reality or inhabit far-off galaxies. Because of this, it really is a rarity to be born as a human being with the unique set of conditions that we have for fulfilling our sacred purpose. Now, whether or not you believe in other dimensions of reality or life in other galaxies, following the strategies outlined up to this point can give you a felt sense of the preciousness of being human.

When you realize that your awareness or Spirit comes through your human form, and when you can look at this from a vast perspective that transcends the small self, you will naturally experience the preciousness of your human body and mind. It becomes apparent how incredibly fortunate you are to be who you are, a sentient being that is capable of recognizing its inseparability from life itself.

2 **The preciousness of being who you uniquely are.** Not only do you feel a general appreciation for being born as a human being, you actually recognize the preciousness of your unique set of attributes, qualities, and even eccentricities. A purposeful person is one who fully and humbly appreciates their unique constellation of experiences that make them who they are. They often exude a quiet confidence, an aura of being fully settled in their own skin, fully okay with who they are. Recognizing your own preciousness is really a way of acknowledging your fundamental completeness at this particular phase of your journey.

When something is precious, it means that it is nearing perfection. Think of a precious diamond or stone. The reason that it is valued so highly is because it has no flaws. At your core, you have the same quality of preciousness. There is nothing to improve upon because, ultimately, there is nothing wrong with you. You have every right to own this and focus on it and to confidently step into the role of someone who expresses this inner preciousness all the time. A purposeful person chooses to live from this perspective and is committed to this above all else. The irony is that this is where true humility comes from. You have to own the preciousness of your nature in order to experience both confidence and humility.

3 **The preciousness of life itself.** Einstein said that the most important decision we make is whether we believe we live in a friendly or hostile universe. When we experience the preciousness of life itself, however, we have moved beyond a belief in good or bad, friendly or hostile. We see that life is empty of any dualistic categories. The universe is never one thing to the exclusion of the other. Everything that happens to us and within us is the same way. Everything is empty, which means its actual essence can't be pinned down by what we think about it.

When we go beyond belief in good or bad, and even more so, when we go beyond the dualistic confines of our thoughts, we can experience the preciousness of life itself. The fact that any of this is here at all is miraculous beyond comprehension. How easy it is to lose track of the basic wonder of life when we are stuck in the small self.

Nothing is fixed, solid, or permanent. Everything is always changing. The law of impermanence is really what makes life so precious. We simply don't know how long we have on this planet, nor do we know how long this planet has. When we fully realize this, every moment becomes precious. There is no time to waste and no moment to ignore. Every single thought, whether good or bad, is impermanent. Whether we're sick or healthy, in a job that we hate or one that we love—all of it will sooner or later fade out of existence. There is a preciousness in this realization, a kind of owning up to the immediacy of this moment. It always harkens back to the same basic idea, which is our first definition of purpose: an awareness of present moment reality. Now is all we have, and when we are fully aware of this moment, we gain access to a reality that is unlimited in its preciousness and sacredness.

This leads us to our last strategy: using the reality of death to live a fuller life. This strategy will expand on this law of impermanence and help you to perceive death in a new and freeing light, which really is the ultimate fruition of the Purpose Principle.

USE THE REALITY OF DEATH TO LIVE A FULLER LIFE

Dying is nothing to fear. It can be the most wonderful experience of your life. It all depends on how you have lived.

Elisabeth Kubler-Ross

It is only fitting that we conclude with the topic that truly is the greatest teacher we have: death.

In order to experience the ultimate freedom that arises as the Purpose Principle comes to fruition, you must have a clear acceptance and understanding of this mysterious force that eludes the grasp of the logical mind.

Throughout this series of strategies, we have made mention of two vastly different aspects of who we are: the small self that lives in the cramped reality of a pebble that does not perceive the infinite space around it, and the Self that is based on life purpose and that knows no limits or boundaries to who or what it is. Let's look at how the small self perceives death and then contrast that with a discussion of what it means to live and die with purpose.

THE SMALL SELF'S VIEW ON DEATH

The small self is doggedly determined to maintain the status quo, avoid change, and cling to whatever security it knows. It has no interest in being spiritually accountable to this life. It wants to hide, to remain veiled in layers of distraction, habit, addiction, familiarity, and false beliefs. Not surprisingly, the small self is absolutely terrified of death. It sees death as an unwelcome and cruel extinction, one that leads to an eternal snuffing out of existence.

The small self views death as the ultimate validation of its cherished beliefs. After all, if we have to die, then life can't be safe, God can't be fair, I can never be enough, I'd better work really, really hard to leave my mark, and so on. It uses death as the primary excuse for self-protection. The problem is that the small self knows that it cannot escape death. Sure, it does its best to pretend that death isn't relevant to it. It lives in a way that has no regard for the natural law of change. Every so often, however, an eruption is created in our way of living that shows the small self that its attempts at control and certainty are ill-fated and misguided. When the small self senses this, it feels conflicted. It works harder to create more problems that make life seem a certain way so as to try to gain more control. Then life presents it with yet another wake-up call, which generates even deeper conflict.

If we live in this way, then our death can only be more of the same process. We will bring more resistance to the dying process than any past event because we see death as the ultimate enemy. We will feel alone and afraid. When we don't learn the sacred strategies outlined here, this is the inevitable outcome of life.

DYING WITH PURPOSE

To die with purpose, we have to live with purpose. So, in a very real way, we can prepare for a liberating, expansive, even wonderful death by choosing to live with purpose starting right now. This purpose-based place that is our real nature has no self-concern. It is basically liberated energy that is here to help others. It does not see death as an enemy or some final outcome, but as another stage of the infinite and eternal process of the universe. There is no small "I" to get bound up in feelings of fear and separation. Rather, we become unified with the cosmic nature of life and death.

Many of the ancient wisdom traditions throughout human history assure us that death can be a liberating and magical process that is in no way the end of our existence. These traditions suggest that death is but another transition into a new form of reality. This realization becomes apparent when our awareness is heightened enough to have a direct experience of the transitory nature of each moment. When our consciousness has shifted to a higher and deeper perspective, we see that there is a death in every moment since life is always changing and giving birth to what is new. When we awaken to this truth, which is most directly encountered in deep states of meditation, prayer, or life-defining events, we see that the death of the physical body is but a transition of our consciousness into another level of being. There is nothing to fear. In fact, we can cultivate an attitude of tremendous curiosity, even excitement, for the great mystery that awaits us beyond our physical body.

These ancient wisdom traditions have long understood a universal truth that our modern world is reluctant to embrace: We are not our bodies. When we live with purpose, we understand this. We are identified with a much more vast presence that goes beyond the material world. When our small self is guiding us, however, we cling to the physical world as the ONLY reality, which is what our cultural conditioning continually reinforces. When the physical body dies, we are forever extinguished. How can we truly believe that our life has a sacred purpose when we will at some undetermined point in the future fade into eternal blackness? That belief does not exactly set the stage for a life of abundance and joy.

In reality, we have the opportunity to die with purpose in each moment. After all, in every second, there is a quality of death. Every thought that moves through our mind, every breath that moves in and out of our diaphragm, every interaction we have with someone, really every single flicker of energy that arises inside and outside of us, is continually arising and passing away. Because of this, we have access to the reality of death in every moment. Experiencing death in this way starting right now is a wonderful preparation for our physical death. It grounds us in the fact that leaving our physical body is just another aspect of change. When we get this, we no longer see death as the enemy. In fact, we can embrace impermanence as being a law of the universe that enables us to see the preciousness of each moment. Even the death of the physical body is precious and sacred.

The teachings of these ancient wisdom traditions are corroborated by many accounts of people who have had near-death experiences. Almost without exception, these accounts describe an overwhelming presence of pure peace and light. Many have described this as a feeling of ultimate safety, as if the universe is penetrating the person's consciousness with unimaginable love. This is why near-death experiences are one of the most profound catalysts to awaken purpose. Many people who return from this experience are immediately and profoundly transformed. They instantly embark on a more authentic course in life that brings them closer to the revelations they experienced as they glimpsed death.

According to the ancient wisdom traditions, each of us has this experience when we die. We are met with a state of unconditional love that completely shatters any narrow perceptions we held on to during our life. If we have cultivated a familiarity with this state of being during our life (through heightening our consciousness and focusing on our purpose), then we will be able to dwell in this state without resistance. If, however, we have identified primarily with the small self during our life, then we will recoil in fear and turn away from the groundlessness and intensity of this universal love as we die. We will identify with the fear that we never resolved during our life. Whatever our day-to-day experience was during life, it is now magnified a billion times when we die because we no longer have the solid reference point of our physical body to shield us from the rawness and enormity of the cosmos. We die how we live—yet another reason to release any obstacles to purpose and joy right now!

DEATH AS A REMINDER

There is nothing that can shake us out of our small self more abruptly than experiencing the death of a loved one. Whether it's a close friend, pet, or family member, the death of someone we care about is a powerful reminder to be fully present to our own life experience right now. The process of grieving is often a way of coming to terms with our own ability to be fully alive. When we lose a loved one, we will often reflect on questions such as:

- ⊙ Was I fully there for them?
- ⊙ Did I love them fully?
- ⊙ Did I show them who I really was?
- ⊙ Did I see who they really were?
- ⊙ Did I do everything I could to help them live the best life possible?
- ⊙ Do I have any regrets?

To the extent that we recognize what we "should" have done for that person, the grieving process is much more pronounced. This puts us face to face with how we are living right now. Are we currently offering the people we love our full Self? Are we sharing our purpose with those that matter most to us?

Indeed, death is a reminder to always keep in mind the preciousness of every detail of our lives. When we experience the death of another, we brush up against our own impermanence. We get hit on a heart level with the fact that, just like the person who passed away, we will no longer be here at some point. Given that the time of our death is entirely uncertain, we feel compelled to embrace the fullness of each moment. In this way, we are always keeping the end in mind. We use the reality of death as an opportunity to become more alive rather than to recoil in fear of the unknown. Rather than perceiving this as an exercise in morbidity, we realize that comprehending our own impermanence is the only gateway we have to heightened consciousness and a life of fulfillment and true abundance.

THE GREATEST DANGER WE FACE

While most of us have been taught that death is the most threatening and dangerous element of life, there is actually something that is immeasurably more harmful and damaging in its consequences: *not being fully alive.* Everything you have learned up to this point has provided you with a wonderful opportunity to wake up and embrace the totality of who you are. You cannot choose to bypass death, but you can choose to ignite your purpose into action right now to become fully alive. You can choose to stop feeding your small self by attaching to self-perceptions that do not serve you or others. You can choose to stop making excuses or acting as if your life doesn't really matter. Making this fundamental choice is the only true refuge we have from suffering. When we choose the opposite—to stay half-asleep—we will remain victims of the whims of fate. Life will knock us around endlessly. Now that is a dangerous situation!

If we refer to the ancient wisdom traditions again, it is widely claimed that the dying process brings us to a heightened state of lucidity and clarity. We experience what is often called a life review, where we flash upon the entire progression of our life experience, from the moment of conception all the way through every instant we have lived. We see with crystal clarity how purposeful our life has been. We see the areas that we chose to stay in our comfort zone out of fear and we see with illuminating precision the extent to which our personal obstacles have held us back. The dying process is an invitation into truth. There is no hiding or deception. The small self is completely exposed for what it is and we see how much virtue and goodness we have showered upon the world. We see what kind of legacy we are leaving behind. When we come face to face with the raw truth of our life, we can die with a quality of profound regret or liberation. It all depends on the seeds we have planted in each moment along the way.

THE ULTIMATE FRUITION

When you look at death from this perspective, it may motivate you to immediately make the choices that will lead to the most enriching, helpful, and prosperous life possible, even if it feels frightening. When you put your purpose first, you are stating to the universe that you are no longer afraid of death. The obstacles to purpose that you have put up with to this point are simply no longer appealing to you. You want the real deal, even if it means suspending everything you believe to be true. You are ready to jump into the unknown. Not only are you ready, you are seriously interested in what you'll find there. Just as you did with so many moments of your life, you focus on bringing space to the dying process by practicing nonresistance. You bring your mind to a place of exquisite curiosity, ready to take the plunge into the Great Mystery.

I have intentionally used the following case study to highlight the death of the small self as opposed to the process of actual physical death. Not only will this help to tie in all the strategies of this book, but it will enable you to see death in a new light.

CASE STUDY ⚜ ASHLEY ⚜

A stay-at-home mom with two young children, Ashley had an opening into her purpose after a rather startling experience she had while shopping at the local mall. She had gone into a dressing room to try on a new pair of jeans and when she looked in the mirror to see if the jeans fit well, she was overcome by a feeling of complete uncertainty and groundlessness. She simply did not recognize the person who was looking back at her. It was as if a complete stranger was reflected in that mirror. At the same time, she was overtaken by a feeling of being completely fed up with everything in her life, from her body to her never-ending role as a caretaker to the incessant worry and anxiety that plagued her every waking thought.

In a moment, Ashley felt her sense of self dissolve. The life that she had known and the role that she had come to play felt not only unnatural, but completely foreign. In an instant, her entire worldview was altered. She was shaken to her core by an almost palpable feeling of death, as she recognized the illusion upon which her life had been built. All of the ways that she had tried to gain control and feel safe had crumbled before her. She was now left looking back at this body in the mirror, completely at a loss as to who this person was or why she was really here.

This was the beginning of a profound transformation for Ashley, as she spent the next seven days doing very little except sitting on her couch, quietly reflecting on her life. She allowed herself to be present with the ongoing feeling that she was dying. In reality, she was basically watching

continued

her small self die. She became fully aware of the daily momentum of her life that kept her at a distance from her purpose-based Self. Ashley experienced a state of total and complete surrender—of who she thought she was, who she should be, and what direction she was going in life. She described this quality of surrender as a state of deep prayer in which she was asking the universe to reveal her true purpose. As she brought a tremendous amount of space to her beliefs about who she was, she could literally feel this small, cramped version of herself dissolving into that space.

As Ashley awakened to the Purpose Principle, every single facet of her life underwent a radical change. Ashley had been addicted to exercise and was running about 25–30 miles per week, which was slowly causing her body to deteriorate with symptoms such as knee and low back pain, shin splints, a bunion, and inflammation in her ankles. She ran this much because she was fixated on shedding that elusive fifteen pounds that had accumulated since giving birth to her two children. Even with such a strict exercise regimen, Ashley could not lose the extra weight. In fact, she was actually gaining weight the more she ran.

After sitting in quiet reflection for seven days, Ashley cut back about 90% on her running. Instead, she began a deep relationship with a restorative yoga practice, which she found to be much healthier for her body and mind.

Ashley had also struggled with a chronic sugar addiction that had become quite severe since having children. After allowing in her purpose, Ashley began to make the connection between her harmful belief that she was

continued

never enough and her compulsive craving for sweets. As a result of this and her more balanced exercise regimen, Ashley lost the extra fifteen pounds almost effortlessly.

Ashley also brought her purpose-based Self to her parenting. Whereas before she was consumed with initiating endless activities and play dates for her kids, Ashley took a newfound interest in simply being with her children. She cut way back on the huge to-do list and committed to bringing her full presence and attention to her children.

Ashley also went through a radical change in her marriage. She had been with her spouse for 12 years prior to her opening into purpose. Within a couple of months after this initial opening, Ashley knew that most of her life had been built on compromise and "should." This was apparent in her marriage, as she realized that she had devoted most of her energy to trying to make the marriage better so she could enjoy a perfect life as a wife and mother. Now, all that she saw was the evidence in front of her that assured her the marriage had holes in the foundation that had always been there. She realized that, although most people would assume she had a perfectly fine marriage, she was starving emotionally in the relationship and that she always had been.

Ashley knew in her heart that she wanted more than this. Even though it would have been more convenient to stay in the marriage, she followed her purpose-based aspirations that were telling her not to compromise any aspect of her life. Because of this, she was able to initiate a healthy separation from her spouse that created more freedom for each of them.

continued

As Ashley began to discover her identity outside of the role of wife and mother, an explosive burst of creative energy welled up within her. Through writing, she recovered a reservoir of creativity that helped to capture her deepest emotions that had been buried under years of suppressing who she really was.

In each of these areas of her life, Ashley experienced the death of what was familiar to her. She literally had to reinvent herself and the life she had created based on her commitment to her life purpose. Even though she had awakened into a higher state of consciousness and wellness, she also went through a grieving process of leaving behind her old ways of being. In many ways, her entry into purpose felt like the death of an old friend.

Ashley had the direct experience of the fact that there is a death and rebirth in every single moment. In order for her purpose to be born, her old ways of being had to die. Committing to her purpose meant facing the consequences of allowing her small self to die. By moving through the pain of doing so, she was able to give birth to her purpose-based Self.

Even though this may sound far-removed from your current experience, remember that revolutionary change can occur in a moment's time. When you are ready to embrace a life of purpose, that in itself is the ultimate fruition. Glimpsing this for even a moment can change the entire course of your life. It is never too late to have this glimpse. Once you do, then it's a matter of implementing the Purpose Principle into your life on a consistent basis.

As you now know, you can actually use this very day to initiate a purposeful life. You can start preparing for death in this very moment, which is a sacred step to living more fully. Since life is always changing and nothing is solid, we always have the opportunity to surrender to the law of impermanence. This is what the Zen poet Bunan meant when he said,

Die while you're alive
And be absolutely dead.
Then do whatever you want:
It's all good.

Congratulations *for taking the time in your busy life to not only read, but to seriously contemplate each of these 11 strategies as they relate to your own current situation. This is a most precious gift to offer yourself and an encouraging sign that you have access to the innate qualities of generosity and freedom that are really what the Purpose Principle is all about.*

I have seen it happen to so many people and I have been guilty of it too: We try to find a solution to our various life challenges without first creating the right foundation. We turn to all kinds of outside resources to get the help we need without realizing that we have to be aligned with our purpose. Any real solution can only come through awareness of present moment reality and a clear understanding of who we really are and what we really want.

Honestly, you already know everything that you have read in this book. All of these strategies have been written with the intention of speaking to an instinctual and intelligent place within you that is 100% aligned with purpose already. If you have felt an uncanny quality of familiarity with the messages contained in this book, it is because you really do know all of this information and you always have. In fact, you *are* the messages contained in this book. It's just that you've likely forgotten this as a result of the various distractions and obstacles that life has presented you with.

As you now consider what to "do" with the information you have gained here, always remember that your work is about clearing away the obstacles to the purpose that's already within you rather than trying to find meaning and freedom outside of yourself. When you keep this understanding in mind, applying the Purpose Principle to every area of your life becomes a natural, almost effortless process.

Your life is a precious event. You are a sacred being with a purpose to fulfill during your time on this planet. By choosing to let go of the obstacles to purpose and awaken your own consciousness, you have a profound ability to shift the awareness of this entire planet toward a higher, more evolved state of being. When you put your purpose first, it has a positive ripple effect on the entire world. It all starts on an individual level. Don't accept mediocrity and don't just tolerate your life. Choose to live fully and offer the absolute best that is within you.

It really is a beautiful thing to tap into the greatest part of your nature and give wholeheartedly back to life. You now have a step-by-step blueprint in place for embarking on this sacred journey. I encourage you to do this now. After all, this is the only reason why you are here.

INTRODUCTION

1. The ancient wisdom traditions that I have primarily focused on in my own life and study are Buddhism, Taoism, Hinduism, and the mystical sects of Christianity.

2. For the purposes of this book, we will be relying on the following definition of strategy taken from Merriam-Webster's Dictionary: An adaptation or complex of adaptations (as of behavior, metabolism, or structure) that serves or appears to serve an important function in achieving evolutionary success.

THIRD STRATEGY

1. The Biology of Belief: Unleashing the Power of Consciousness, Matter, and Miracles by Bruce Lipton, Ph.D., p. 67.

2. Train Your Mind, Change Your Brain by Sharon Begley, pp. 7–8.

FOURTH STRATEGY

1. Most of these beliefs are excerpted from Christel Nani's book Sacred Choices: Thinking Outside the Tribe to Heal Your Spirit, p. 15.

EIGHTH STRATEGY

1. It's important to remember here that the connection between thoughts, emotions, and physical health is not always immediately apparent or logical. I have had many patients who exhibited very healthy emotional patterns yet were struggling with physical health issues. While I would generally agree that there is typically an intimate link between the nature of one's thoughts and emotions and their physical health, in my clinical experience this is not a hard and fast rule. The interplay between the mind and body is too complex to say that negative thought and emotion is always the cause of physical disease, which is a commonly held theory in holistic medicine.

NINTH STRATEGY

1. If you'd like further guidance with meditation, go to http://www.mindfulness-cd.net and get a copy of my meditation CD, Meditation: Mindfulness Practice for Beginners.

Contact

Kevin Doherty, L.Ac., MS

Phone **303 725 6208**

Web sites

For more information about the book and Kevin's coaching programs:

www.PurposePrinciple.com

www.PurposePrinciple.com/blog

To join Kevin's online membership community, go to

www.PurposePrinciple.com/membership.html

For Acupuncture:

www.BoulderCountyAcupuncture.com

Email **Kevin@PurposePrinciple.com**

For quantity discounts, promotions or sponsorship of *the Purpose Principle*,

please email me at **Kevin@PurposePrinciple.com**

Kevin Doherty is a licensed

acupuncturist, life and business coach, engaging speaker, and entrepreneur. Through his numerous books and workshops, he is a recognized thought leader in the fields of alternative medicine and personal development. Kevin has a private practice in Superior, Colorado where he utilizes a unique combination of acupuncture, life coaching, and meditation instruction. Through these methods, Kevin has successfully treated hundreds of patients for issues ranging from anxiety and depression to chronic pain and hormonal imbalances.

Since 1992 Kevin has dedicated his life to understanding and practicing the following topics:

- Human potential: how people overcome limitations and stagnation to achieve personal greatness
- Life purpose: how people identify their core gifts and bring them out to the world
- The merging of spirituality and entrepreneurship: how to integrate our purpose in a meaningful and authentic way into the conventional world
- The actualization of life freedom: time, money, work, relationships, and health

His decision to coach has been an organic outpouring of the deep commitment he has to help others become fully realized in the context of these life themes. Simply put, it is the form that has enabled his own life purpose to come to fruition.

Kevin offers group and one-on-one coaching to people worldwide based on the strategies he discusses in his book The Purpose Principle.

To learn more, go to **http://www.PurposePrinciple.com**.

LaVergne, TN USA
24 January 2011
213671LV00002B/7/P